Best of
Taste

Flavors
of the
Pacific Coast

JOHN SARICH

SEA·HILL
PRESS

Dedication

To all the cooks, both professional and at home,
who have helped me by sharing their techniques,
insights, ideas, and discoveries; and to all
who share the love of food and wine.

This is a companion book to the television series
Best of Taste: Flavors of the Pacific Coast.
Executive producers: John McLean & Greg Sharp
Director: John Barry
Host: John Sarich
Camera: John Cline
Post production: eln Communications, Seattle, Washington

Published by Sea-Hill Press, Inc.
6101 200th St. SW, Suite 205
Lynnwood, WA 98036
425.697.3606
www.seahillpress.com

Publisher: Greg Sharp
Editor: Cynthia Sharp
Book Design: Barbara Schmitt
Production Assistant: Heather Bauerle
Editorial Assistant: Jamie Trubia
Photography: Christopher Conrad
and Robert Pennington
Photography Assistant: Isobel Alexander

All recipes include U.S. and metric measures. Metric conversions
are based on a standard developed for this book. Actual weights may vary.

ISBN 0-9708050-0-4
Sarich, John
Best of Taste: Flavors of the Pacific Coast

Printed in Hong Kong

Table of Contents

Introduction

One of the greatest advantages to living on the Pacific Coast is the amazing convergence of cultures. From Alaska to Mexico, and from the Far East to Australia and on to California, the Pacific Coast boasts a wide availability of ingredients and styles that can be combined in ever-shifting forms. The wildly diverse makeup of the Pacific Coast region, long blessed by strong currents of immigration, contributes not only a highly influential Asian cuisine, but also European technique and Southwestern style. Chefs on the coast do well to incorporate all of these, including the fabulous array of fresh local ingredients, to create fusion cuisine that often applies European method to Asian ingredients, or vice versa.

Cultural cuisine blending can be found in recipes within this book, and is exemplified by the Seared Sea Scallops with

Wasabi Cream. The wine and cream reduction sauce described in this recipe is a classic Old World technique, but is spiced by the Japanese wasabi and used to flavor Alaskan scallops. Similarly, the Pacific Rim Style Crab and Vermicelli mixes flavors of Vietnam and Thailand with fresh Dungeness crab, a Northwest specialty. Even southwestern style gets mixed into Pacific Northwest fare, notably by dishes such as Brine-Soaked Pork Loin, paired with Red Beans and Rice. This dish is of course a Mexican staple, updated with local ingredients.

The presence of south-of-the-border influence in the Northwest is evidenced by the popularity of restaurants such as Chef Christine Keff's "Fandango," which focuses on merging the cuisine of Mexico and the Americas with the Pacific Northwest.

Chefs cooking along the Pacific Coast have the advantage of not only a mass of cultural influences to choose from, but also a bounty of fresh and delicious ingredients to use. When thinking of creating a meal, one must think not only of the style and flavor of the dish, but also the season. When you use only the freshest ingredients available, you have to constantly change your menu, so you can be sure to always have the most varied fare in town. From dairy, meat, and seafood, to vegetables, grain, and spices, the Pacific Coast's availability of ingredients is second to none. It is part of the joy of cooking to use this advantage to its fullest.

The beautiful waters of the Pacific Ocean teem with incredible variety and provide a rich harvest from the sea.

In my position I travel frequently, all around the world, and am heavily influenced by each region that I visit. Wherever I go, I always keep the Pacific Coast staples in mind. But I am also shaped by my own Croatian heritage, so even my West Coast recipes have a Mediterranean touch. The "abodanza," or abundance, of ingredients and styles of food to choose from makes me, and you, very lucky.

To top it off, this region produces some of the finest wines in the world that only make the food taste better. To get the most pleasure out of cooking for your friends and family, keep the recipes simple, but the flavors full, and enjoy all of the treasures of the Pacific Coast.

Food and Wine

For the 24 years that I've been in the food and wine profession, the pleasure of matching friends, food, and wine has always been the most enjoyable part. I'm often asked what wine goes with what food, and what food goes with what wine. After all these years I've found that there is no one answer. Of course, the old standard of pairing white wine with white meat and seafood, and red wine with red meat is still quite helpful. But when creating a meal there are many other factors to take into consideration.

Another way to look at wine and food pairing is to match similar flavors. For example, you might pair a rich, creamy dish to a rich, creamy Chardonnay. Or spicy foods, such as many Asian dishes, could be matched with an equally spicy wine like a Riesling. There are always exceptions to these rules. One of the easy ways to follow this particular idea is to think of the overall flavors—lighter flavored foods would go with lighter wines, and fuller foods match full wines. You could perhaps even reverse this concept by pairing contrasting flavors. Try this by matching a heavy cream sauce with a light, crisp Sauvignon Blanc or a Pinot Gris. Either way, you

are thinking about flavor, both of the food and of the wine, and picking a wine based on what you want to emphasize about the meal. The most important thing to do is to drink the wine you like with the food you like.

A reliable guide to matching food with wine is to drink the wine that is used in preparing the meal. When cooking with wine, it is vital to use a good quality wine, something that you would enjoy drinking, not a specially labeled "cooking wine." Centuries ago, in European villas and chateaux, salt was added to wine to keep cooks from consuming it before it could be used in meal preparation. Even though the resulting "cooking wine" tasted terrible, the tactic didn't stop the cooks from drinking it!

When serving wine, temperature is the most important factor to keep in mind. White wines must be kept in the refrigerator at 40°F, or less, and consumed at 52-55°F. An easy way to bring the temperature of white wine to the appropriate level is to take the bottle out of the refrigerator 15 to 20 minutes before serving. When white wine gets too cold, the chill masks the bouquet and hides much of what is pleasurable about white wine.

Red wines in general should be served at what is called cellar temperature (64°-66°F), not room temperature. If your wine is stored at room temperature, simply put it in the refrigerator for 15 to 20 minutes.

As for sparkling wines, I prefer mine ice cold! The bubbles release the flavor and bouquet, leaving little for you to do but pour and savor.

When aging wine, it is important to maintain a constant temperature of 64-65°F. The hotter the temperature, the faster the wine ages. When decanting aged red wine, try pouring slowly into a decanter to avoid the sediment, leaving the last bit of wine, along with the sediment, in the bottom of the bottle. You can also take young red wines, like Cabernets and Merlots, and decant them before drinking to aerate and soften the wine. The result will be a softer, more pleasant wine. Wine should be stored on the side, except sparkling wine which should be stored standing up.

There are many areas of the world that make wonderful wines, from the Old World to the Pacific Coast. Keep an open mind when choosing your wines to match your foods.

A delightful selection of premium wines offers a tantalizing dimension to the culinary treats of the Pacific Coast region.

Guide to Food and Wine Pairing

	White Wines			
	Medium Dry		**Dry**	
	Johannisberg Riesling	Gewurztraminer	Pinot Gris	Semillon
Mild Cheeses	✽	✽	✽	✽
Strongly Flavored Cheeses			✽	
Appetizers	✽	✽	✽	✽
Oysters			✽	✽
Shrimp, Crab and Lobster	✽		✽	
Clams and Mussels			✽	✽
Seafood with Wine or Light Sauces	✽		✽	✽
Seafood with Cream Sauces			✽	
Grilled Fish	✽		✽	✽
Salmon				✽
Cream Sauces			✽	✽
Mediterranean-Style Pasta				
Chicken, Turkey and Game Hen	✽	✽	✽	
Pheasant, Duck and Goose		✽		
Asian Cuisine	✽	✽	✽	✽
Pork and Veal		✽		
Lamb				
Game				
Beef				
Fruit and Light Desserts				
Chocolate Desserts				

		Red Wines						Dessert Wines		
Sauvignon Blanc	Chardonnay	Syrah	Pinot Noir	Zinfandel	Cabernet Franc	Merlot / Meritage	Cabernet Sauvignon	Late Harvest White Riesling	Late Harvest Semillon	Port
DRY		MEDIUM-BODIED		FULL-BODIED				SWEET		
❀										
❀	❀	❀	❀	❀	❀	❀	❀	❀	❀	❀
❀		❀								
❀										
❀	❀									
❀										
❀	❀									
	❀									
❀		❀	❀	❀	❀					
	❀	❀	❀	❀		❀				
❀	❀									
		❀	❀	❀	❀	❀	❀			
❀	❀	❀		❀	❀					
	❀	❀	❀	❀	❀	❀				
					❀	❀				
	❀	❀	❀	❀			❀			
	❀		❀	❀	❀	❀	❀			
	❀	❀	❀	❀	❀	❀	❀			
		❀			❀	❀	❀			
								❀	❀	❀
						❀	❀			

Appetizers

Avocado Stuffed with Shrimp

*I had a dish similar to this back in 1970 at The Palace Hotel
in San Francisco. This is a take-off on that dish.*

Serves 4

2 avocados, halved and meat
  removed (save shell)
$^1/_2$ pound (225 g) small cooked
  shrimp
1 clove garlic, mashed
2 tablespoons chopped cilantro
Pinch cayenne pepper

1 teaspoon chili powder
Juice of $^1/_2$ lemon
Salt to taste
$^1/_4$ cup (57 g) mayonnaise
2 tablespoons Chardonnay
2 tablespoons grated Jack cheese
Fresh salsa, for serving

Preheat oven to 350°F (180°C). Lightly mash avocados and
mix with remaining ingredients, except cheese. Stuff back into empty
shells. Bake for 15 to 20 minutes. Top with grated Jack cheese and
return to oven until cheese has melted. Serve with fresh salsa.

Chef's Notes:

*When selecting wines to go with appetizers,
remember that sparkling wines are always great
with lighter dishes. For variety, you can also
offer a Riesling or Chardonnay.*

WINE
RECOMMENDATION:

Chardonnay

Tuscan Chicken Liver Paté on Crostini

Upon traveling to Tuscany I was delighted to discover that this dish is quite popular throughout the region.

Serves 4 to 6

2 cloves garlic, mashed
4 shallots, finely chopped
2 tablespoons butter
1 pound (450 g) chicken livers
2 tablespoons Sauvignon Blanc
1 teaspoon sherry vinegar

$^1/_4$ teaspoon chopped fresh sage
Pinch cayenne pepper
Salt to taste
White pepper to taste
Crostini, for serving

Sauté garlic and shallots in butter over medium-high heat until soft, about 5 minutes. Add chicken livers and sauté another 6 minutes, stirring frequently. Add Sauvignon Blanc, sherry vinegar, sage, cayenne pepper, salt, and white pepper. Cook another 5 minutes. Cool. Place in a food processor or blender and blend until smooth. Spread on crostini and serve.

Chef's Notes:

Crostini means "little toasts" in Italian. They are simply small, thin slices of toasted bread. They can be prepared at home or bought at the grocery store. You can brush a bit of olive oil or butter on them if you'd like, or just top them with paté.

WINE
RECOMMENDATION:

Sauvignon Blanc
or
Pinot Gris

Crab-Stuffed Mushrooms
Serves 6 to 8

1 pound (450 g) crab meat
8 ounces (225 g) cream cheese
2 tablespoons mayonnaise
2 tablespoons lemon juice
2 tablespoons finely diced
  red bell pepper

$1/2$ teaspoon dry mustard
Salt to taste
White pepper to taste
Mushroom caps, raw or steamed
  and cooled

Mix together all ingredients except mushrooms. Stuff mushroom caps with the filling and serve.

Eggplant and Mushrooms on Crostini
Serves 6 to 8

2 tablespoons olive oil
Juice of 1 lemon
2 tablespoons Sauvignon Blanc
2 to 3 cloves garlic, mashed
2 tablespoons chopped fresh basil
2 tablespoons chopped fresh
  oregano
2 tablespoons chopped fresh
  Italian parsley
$1/8$ teaspoon cumin

$1/8$ teaspoon paprika
$1/2$ teaspoon dry mustard
Pinch red pepper flakes
Salt and pepper to taste
1 pound (450 g) medium
  mushrooms, cleaned
  and quartered
1 eggplant (aubergine),
  cut into $1/2$" (1.25 cm) cubes
Crostini, to serve

Mix together all ingredients except mushrooms, eggplant, and crostini. Marinate mushrooms and eggplant in the mixture for 1 hour. Drain mushrooms and eggplant. Sauté quickly in a very hot skillet until just brown. Serve on crostini.

WINE
RECOMMENDATION:

*Johannisberg
Reisling
or
Sauvignon Blanc*

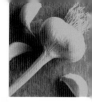

Lox and Melon

Serves 6 to 8

$^1/_2$ pound (225 g) lox-style smoked
  salmon
1 cantaloupe or honeydew melon
  (muskmelon), scooped into balls

1 lime, cut into small wedges

Wrap a slice of lox around each melon ball, place a lime wedge on top or squeeze lime juice over top if preferred, and secure with a toothpick.

Smoked Salmon and Cream Cheese Spread

Serves 6 to 8

1 pound (450 g) cream or
  fresh goat cheese, softened
$^1/_2$ cup (113 g) smoked salmon
1 tablespoon mayonnaise

1 teaspoon capers
$^1/_2$ teaspoon chopped fresh dill
1 clove garlic, mashed
Squeeze of lemon juice

Mix all ingredients together thoroughly and refrigerate for 1 hour. Serve as a spread.

Wine
Recommendation:

*Blanc de Blanc
Sauvignon Blanc
or
Dry Riesling*

Smoked Duck with Dried Cherry Chutney on Crostini

Serves 6 to 8

2 smoked duck breasts,
  finely chopped
1 red onion, finely chopped
2 cloves garlic, finely chopped
1 tablespoon olive oil
2 tablespoons finely chopped
  dried cherries
1 tablespoon chopped fresh
  oregano

1 tablespoon chopped fresh
  Italian parsley
1 tablespoon Dijon mustard
1 tablespoon balsamic vinegar
$1/8$ teaspoon cumin
Freshly ground black pepper
  to taste
$1/8$ teaspoon orange zest
Crostini, for serving

Combine all ingredients except crostini and mix well. The mixture should have the consistency of a thick spread. Spread on crostini and top with cherry chutney, below.

Dried Cherry Chutney

1 cup (225 g) finely chopped
  dried cherries
1 cup (225 g) whole canned
  cranberries
1 red onion, chopped
1 clove garlic, chopped

Pinch ground cloves
1 tablespoon chopped fresh
  Italian parsley
1 tablespoon dry mustard
1 teaspoon honey
1 tablespoon orange juice

Combine all ingredients and use as chutney to serve with crostini.

WINE
RECOMMENDATION:

Merlot

Spot Prawns and Yogurt-Curry Dip

Serves 6 to 8

PRAWNS:
2 quarts (1.9 l) water
$^1/_4$ cup (60 ml) Sauvignon Blanc
3 cloves whole garlic
6 black peppercorns
Juice of $^1/_2$ lemon
Pinch red pepper flakes
Pinch salt
2 pounds (900 g) spot prawns
  or gulf prawns, cleaned,
  peeled, and deveined

YOGURT-CURRY DIP:
$^1/_2$ cup (113 g) yogurt
1 tablespoon mayonnaise
1 tablespoon lemon juice
2 cloves garlic, mashed
$^1/_2$ teaspoon curry powder
Chopped fresh cilantro,
  for garnish

For the prawns, in a saucepan, combine all ingredients except prawns. Bring to a boil and simmer for 10 minutes. Add prawns and cook until tender and color changes to red, about 5 minutes.

For the dip, blend all ingredients and refrigerate until ready to serve. Garnish with cilantro and serve with the prawns.

Chef's Notes:

Indian curry powder can vary greatly depending
on the spices and herbs used in the blend. Look
for a high-quality curry powder. I prefer to use
Madras as it's hotter than the standard style.

WINE
RECOMMENDATION:

Blanc de Blanc
Sparkling Wine
or
Sauvignon Blanc

Stuffed Mediterranean Mussels

Serves 6 to 8

1 tablespoon extra virgin olive oil

1 tablespoon extra virgin olive oil
$^1/_2$ cup (57 g) plain fine
  bread crumbs
2 garlic cloves, mashed
$^1/_3$ cup (42 g) grated Parmesan
  cheese
2 tablespoons finely chopped
  fresh basil
2 tablespoons finely chopped fresh
  Italian parsley

Pinch red pepper flakes
Pinch salt
$^1/_4$ teaspoon dry mustard
2 tablespoons Sauvignon Blanc
Squeeze of fresh lemon
1 dozen mussels, cleaned and
  debearded, steamed open,
  top shell removed

Preheat broiler. Combine all ingredients, except mussels, and mix together well. Top mussels in their shells with filling and place the stuffed mussels in their shells on a baking sheet. Place under broiler and broil until just brown.

Chef's Notes:

To steam mussels: Place mussels in a heavy-bottomed

saucepan. Pour 2 tablespoons of Sauvignon Blanc and

a squeeze of lemon over mussels. Cover and place on

high heat. Cook mussels, shaking the pot occasionally

until they open, about 3 to 4 minutes.

WINE
RECOMMENDATION:

Pinot Gris
or
Sauvignon Blanc

Teriyaki Chicken Wings
Serves 6 to 8

$^1/_4$ cup (60 ml) peanut oil
$^1/_2$ teaspoon sesame oil
2 tablespoons Dry Reisling
2 tablespoons soy sauce
1 tablespoon rice vinegar
1 tablespoon lemon juice
2 tablespoons honey

1 tablespoon chopped ginger
$^1/_2$ tablespoon chopped garlic
1 tablespoon chopped cilantro
1 teaspoon dry mustard
3 pounds (1.35 kg) chicken wings,
   remove tip, divide into
   2 segments at the joint

Mix together all ingredients except chicken wings. Pour over chicken wing segments and marinate 1 hour.

Preheat oven to 350°F (180°C). Bake chicken wings covered for 30 minutes, turning occasionally. Remove cover and bake 30 minutes longer, turning occasionally.

Chef's Notes:

When preparing a selection of appetizers for a
gathering, think about balancing flavors. If you'll
be serving a meal after the appetizers, then it is
best to avoid heavy, high protein dishes.
However, if you're having an appetizer-only event,
then you can think about balancing a heartier
offering like the Tuscan Chicken Liver Paté with
a light dish like Apricot-Ginger Prawns.

WINE
RECOMMENDATION:

Dry Reisling

Roasted Red Pepper and Mushroom-Stuffed Phyllo

This can be served with a veal stock reduction sauce or demi-glace, or alone.

Serves 6 to 8

$1/2$ pound (225 g) chanterelle mushrooms

$1/4$ pound (113 g) oyster mushrooms

$1/4$ pound (113 g) black trumpet mushrooms (if available)

$1/4$ pound (113 g) morel mushrooms

2 tablespoons olive oil

1 medium yellow onion, julienned

1 roasted red bell pepper, julienned

1 roasted yellow bell pepper, julienned

2 cloves garlic, mashed

1 tablespoon chopped fresh oregano

2 tablespoons chopped fresh Italian parsley

1 tablespoon chopped fresh thyme

$1/2$ teaspoon cumin

1 tablespoon balsamic vinegar

Pinch red pepper flakes

1 teaspoon dry mustard

Salt and pepper to taste

$1/4$ cup (30 g) grated Gorgonzola cheese

$1/4$ cup (30 g) grated Parmesan cheese

1 (1 pound/450 g) package phyllo dough

Butter, for brushing phyllo

Chop all mushrooms and set aside. In a skillet, heat olive oil. Sauté onion and bell peppers in olive oil until just tender. Add garlic and mushrooms and sauté quickly over high heat until just tender. Remove from heat and add oregano, parsley, thyme, cumin, balsamic vinegar, red pepper flakes, dry mustard, salt and pepper, Gorgonzola cheese, and Parmesan cheese. Mix together well. Cool.

Preheat oven to 350°F (180°C). Butter a sheet of phyllo, and repeat 2 more times until 3 layers of phyllo have been buttered and layered. Fill with mixture and roll. Bake in oven until brown, about 12 minutes.

WINE RECOMMENDATION:

Sauvignon Blanc
or
Pinot Gris

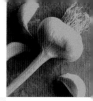

Phyllo Triangles

Serve with a chilled Sauvignon Blanc or a Lightly Oaked Chardonnay.

Serves 6 to 8

1 cup (225 g) ricotta cheese
1 package (10 ounce/285 g) frozen
  chopped spinach, thawed and
  thoroughly squeezed of liquid
2 garlic cloves, chopped
2 tablespoons chopped oil-packed
  sun-dried tomatoes
2 tablespoons pine nuts

4 tablespoons grated Parmesan
  cheese
Salt to taste
$^{1}/_{2}$ cup (118 ml) olive oil
3 egg whites, lightly beaten
1 (1 pound/450 g) package
  phyllo dough

Thoroughly mix together ricotta cheese, spinach, garlic, sun-dried tomatoes, pine nuts, and Parmesan cheese. Add salt to taste.

Preheat oven to 350°F (180°C). In a separate bowl, mix olive oil and egg whites and brush over a sheet of phyllo. Repeat 2 more times until 3 sheets have been brushed and layered. Cut into 6 strips. Place 2 tablespoons of filling at the bottom of each strip and fold end-over-end to make a triangle. Brush top of triangles with oil and egg mixture and bake 7 minutes, or until golden brown.

Turkey with Ginger Chutney

Serves 12

1 (8 ounce/225 g) can whole
  cranberries, drained and
  lightly mashed
2 tablespoons blackberry or
  raspberry preserves

1 tablespoon fresh orange juice
1 teaspoon grated fresh ginger
$1^{1}/_{2}$ pounds (675 g) smoked
  turkey breast, thinly sliced
Toasted French bread rounds

Mix together cranberries, preserves, juice, and ginger and chill for 1 hour. Mound half or whole slice of smoked turkey on toasted French bread round. Top with the ginger chutney. Serve at room temperature.

WINE
RECOMMENDATION:

*Sparkling Wine
or
Riesling*

Polenta with Salmon and Salsa

Serves 12

1 tablespoon olive oil
1 tablespoon butter
2 cloves garlic, finely chopped
2 shallots, finely chopped
1¹/₂ cups (350 ml) chicken stock
2 tablespoons Dry Riesling
2 tablespoons chopped
  smoked salmon
2 tablespoons finely chopped
  green chilies

1 tablespoon finely chopped
  cilantro
¹/₂ teaspoon chili powder
Salt to taste
1 cup (225 g) fine cornmeal
Sour cream, for garnish
Salsa, for garnish

In a skillet, heat olive oil and butter and quickly sauté garlic and shallots. Add stock and bring to a simmer. Add Dry Riesling, salmon, green chilies, cilantro, chili powder, and salt. Add cornmeal, stirring constantly until smooth and tender. Remove from heat and pour into a buttered 17" x 11" (27.5 x 17.5 cm) baking pan. Cool in refrigerator for 1 hour or overnight. Turn upside down and cut into wedges. Serve with sour cream and salsa.

WINE
RECOMMENDATION:

Riesling

Potato and Salmon Pancakes with Caviar

Serves 12

3 medium russet potatoes, peeled, boiled, and mashed
3 egg yolks
2 egg whites, lightly beaten
1/4 cup (60 ml) whipping cream
2 tablespoons flour
4 cloves garlic, roasted (see Chef's Notes)

2 tablespoons chopped fresh dill
Salt and pepper to taste
2 tablespoons butter
1 small jar black caviar
12 thin slices lox-style salmon
Sour cream, for garnish
1 small jar salmon caviar

After mashing potatoes, cool and then add egg yolks. Beat egg yolks into mashed potatoes. Add egg whites and cream and mix well. Add flour, garlic, and dill. Add salt and pepper to taste. The mixture should resemble thick pancake batter.

In a skillet on medium-high heat, melt butter. Pour 1/4 cup of potato mixture into the skillet as you would in making pancakes. When pancake is brown on first side, turn over.

Top with 1/2 teaspoon black caviar, and 1 piece of lox, and cook about 1 1/2 minutes longer. Remove from pan and top with a dollop of sour cream and 1/2 teaspoon salmon caviar.

Chef's Notes:

I like to slow roast garlic in the oven. To do this, trim the top of a garlic bulb, but leave the cloves intact. Place trimmed garlic on a sheet of tin foil, and sprinkle with olive oil, salt, and freshly ground black pepper. Bake in a pre-heated 350°F (180°C) oven for 30 minutes. Well-roasted garlic will be extremely soft, and have a paste-like consistency.

WINE RECOMMENDATION:

Sparkling Wine Blanc de Blanc or Riesling

Apricot-Ginger Prawns
Serves 6

1 tablespoon grated fresh ginger
$^1/_2$ cup (118 ml) orange juice
$^1/_2$ teaspoon peanut oil
$^1/_8$ teaspoon sesame oil
$^1/_2$ teaspoon rice vinegar
2 tablespoons Johannisberg
  Riesling

1 tablespoon light soy sauce
$^1/_2$ cup (113 g) apricot preserves
2 tablespoons chopped fresh
  cilantro
1 pound (450 g) (16 to 20 count)
  prawns, peeled and deveined

In a saucepan combine ginger, orange juice, peanut oil, sesame oil, rice vinegar, wine, soy sauce, apricot preserves, and cilantro. Bring to a simmer. Cook for 5 to 10 minutes, until slightly thickened. Thread prawns on skewers and grill, basting frequently with the sauce, until their color has changed to bright red and white.

Chef's Notes:

I use very small amounts of oil in most of my recipes. Oil carries flavor and if a flavorful oil is used, very little is needed. If a dish is made with fresh ingredients, you don't want to hide the flavor by overdoing the fat content.

WINE
RECOMMENDATION:

*Johannisberg
Riesling*

Apricot-Ginger Prawns

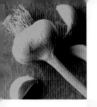

Seared Sea Scallops with Wasabi Cream

Serves 12

Salt and pepper to taste
36 large sea scallops
1 tablespoon butter
1 tablespoon peanut oil
2 large shallots, thinly sliced
1 garlic clove, mashed
$^1/_4$ teaspoon grated fresh ginger
$^1/_4$ cup (60 ml) Sauvignon Blanc
$^1/_4$ cup (60 ml) chicken stock

$^1/_3$ cup (80 ml) heavy cream
$^1/_2$ teaspoon prepared wasabi
(Asian green horseradish)
Squeeze lemon juice
Salt to taste
Orange or red flying fish roe,
for garnish
Cilantro sprigs, for garnish

Lightly salt and pepper the sea scallops. In a large skillet, heat butter and oil together until very hot and sear scallops in batches until brown on both sides. Remove to a warm platter. Drain any liquid remaining in the pan the scallops were cooked in, and add shallots, garlic, and ginger and sauté until soft. Add Sauvignon Blanc and chicken stock, and simmer until reduced by half. Add cream and simmer till mixture thickens. Turn heat to low and whisk in wasabi and a squeeze of lemon juice. Add salt to taste. Spoon sauce onto a plate, place scallops on top, and top with a little orange or red flying fish roe and sprigs of cilantro for garnish.

WINE
RECOMMENDATION:

Sauvignon Blanc
or
Lightly Oaked
Chardonnay

Seared Sea Scallops with Wasabi Cream

Soups and Salads

Asian Slaw Salad with Smoked Duck Breast and Ginger-Plum Chutney

The chutney and the slaw salad are both tasty served either hot or cold, and the chutney is also great over grilled or smoked meat. Sauté or stir the chutney ingredients together—I like it either way, so the choice is yours.

Serves 4 to 6

GINGER-PLUM CHUTNEY:
1 small red onion, diced
1/8 teaspoon grated fresh ginger
1 teaspoon peanut oil
1 tablespoon rice wine vinegar
1 cup (225 g) diced fresh plums
Pinch cayenne
Pinch salt

3 carrots, julienned
$^1/_2$ cup (113 g) julienned snow peas
1 cup (225 g) julienned jicama, peeled
1 cup (225 g) julienned shiitake mushrooms
1 tablespoon rice vinegar
1 tablespoon soy sauce

SLAW SALAD:
2 tablespoons peanut oil, divided
Splash sesame oil
2 cloves garlic, sliced
1 teaspoon grated ginger
1 cup (225 g) julienned Napa cabbage

DUCK:
1 head Bibb (butter) lettuce leaves arranged into "cups"
$1^1/_2$ cups (340 g) julienned smoked duck breast
Chopped fresh cilantro, for garnish

For the chutney, toss ingredients together and let stand for at least an hour before serving, but preferably overnight.

If you prefer, in a saucepan, briefly sauté onion and ginger in peanut oil. Add remaining ingredients and stir. When plums are just heated through, remove from heat. Serve immediately, or cool and store for future use.

For the duck salad, heat 1 tablespoon peanut oil, sesame oil, garlic, and ginger in a large saucepan. Add cabbage, carrots, peas, jicama, and mushrooms. Sauté over high heat until just wilted, about 2 minutes. Remove from heat and toss with rice vinegar, remaining peanut oil, and soy sauce. Place in lettuce cups and top with smoked duck breast, chutney, and cilantro.

Balsamic Dressing

$^1/_4$ cup (60 ml) balsamic vinegar
$^1/_2$ cup (118 ml) extra virgin
  olive oil
1 clove garlic, mashed
Pinch sugar

Pinch salt
$^1/_4$ teaspoon dry mustard
Generous amount freshly ground
  black pepper

Mix all ingredients together and toss with salad greens.

Creamy Lemon Dijon Dressing

Juice of 1 lemon
$^1/_8$ teaspoon sugar
$^1/_2$ teaspoon chopped capers
2 anchovy fillets or squirt
  (1 teaspoon) anchovy paste
2 tablespoons sherry vinegar

Salt to taste
1 tablespoon Dijon mustard
$^1/_2$ cup (118 ml) extra virgin
  olive oil
1 clove garlic, mashed

Mix all ingredients well and let stand for 30 minutes. Serve over salad greens.

Chef's Notes:

*Since salads act as a palate cleanser, much like
wine, most salads stand alone. Acids, like lemon
and vinegar, can make wine flat and tannic.*

Wasabi-Soy Vinaigrette

Use this Wasabi Soy Vinaigrette as a dipping sauce for freshly shucked oysters. It also works well as a dressing for a refreshing salad of grated carrot, jicama, snow peas, and water chestnuts.

1 teaspoon prepared wasabi
1 tablespoon soy sauce
1 tablespoon rice vinegar
$^1/_2$ teaspoon finely chopped
  fresh cilantro

1 clove garlic, mashed
$^1/_2$ teaspoon grated fresh ginger
$^1/_8$ teaspoon red chili paste

Mix all ingredients together. Serve with freshly shucked oysters.

Bibb Lettuce with Lemon Salad

Serves 4

1 head Bibb (butter) lettuce
2 small tomatoes, quartered
1 tablespoon coarsely chopped
  fresh basil
$1^1/_2$ tablespoons extra virgin
  olive oil

1 tablespoon lemon juice
Pinch sugar
Salt to taste
Freshly ground black pepper
  to taste

Gently tear Bibb lettuce leaves and arrange in a bowl. Top with tomatoes and fresh basil. Mix olive oil, lemon juice, sugar, and salt to taste. Pour dressing over salad. Finish with freshly ground black pepper to taste.

Mixed Wild Green Salad with Goat Cheese

Serves 4

GREENS:

¹/₂ pound (225 g) mixed wild greens
1 roasted red bell pepper,
  peeled and julienned
1 roasted yellow bell pepper,
  peeled and julienned
1 fennel bulb, very thinly julienned
1 small red onion, julienned
Freshly ground black pepper
¹/₂ pound (225 g) goat cheese,
  crumbled

DRESSING:

2 tablespoons balsamic vinegar
¹/₄ cup (60 ml) extra virgin olive oil
2 cloves garlic, mashed
¹/₈ teaspoon dry mustard
1 teaspoon chopped fresh basil
1 teaspoon chopped fresh oregano
Pinch salt

For the greens, arrange wild greens on a plate and top with bell peppers, fennel, and onion. Sprinkle with black pepper and crumbled goat cheese.

For the dressing, whisk all ingredients together and drizzle over greens.

Chef's Notes:

*Match red wines, such as Zinfandel, Syrah, and Merlot
with Cambenzola, Stilton, Gorgonzola or Danish blue
cheeses. White wines, such as Sauvignon Blanc and Pinot
Gris, go wonderfully with young fresh goat cheese,
marinated with extra virgin olive oil and chopped basil
leaves; young pecorino, and French or Israeli feta cheese.*

Ginger-Curry Pumpkin Soup
Serves 4 to 6

4 pounds (1.8 kg) pumpkin,
  cleaned and quartered
2 tablespoons butter
Salt and pepper to taste
1 large onion, chopped
2 cloves garlic, chopped
1 tablespoon chopped fresh ginger
1 tablespoon peanut oil

1 teaspoon curry powder
2 tablespoons Riesling
4 cups (946 ml) chicken broth
Salt to taste
Sour cream, for garnish
2 tablespoons chopped fresh
  cilantro, for garnish

Preheat oven to 350°F (180°C). Place pumpkin on a baking sheet and spread with butter. Sprinkle with salt and pepper. Bake in oven for 30 minutes, or until fork tender. Remove from oven and let cool. Scrape the flesh from the skin, discard the skin and set the flesh aside.

In a large saucepan, sauté onion, garlic, and ginger in peanut oil until soft. Add curry powder and cook a few more minutes to release the flavor of the curry. Add wine and chicken broth and simmer 3 or 4 minutes. Stir in pumpkin and add salt to taste. In a blender, blend soup until smooth. Pour into bowls and garnish with a small scoop of sour cream and fresh cilantro.

WINE
RECOMMENDATION:

*Riesling
or
Sauvignon Blanc*

Oyster Twist

Serves 4

1 onion, julienned
2 medium or 4 baby leeks, thinly
  sliced
2 tablespoons butter
6 finger (baby long whites) or
  Yukon gold potatoes, quartered
1 clove garlic, mashed
$^1/_2$ cup (118 ml) chicken stock
2 tablespoons Chardonnay

$^1/_3$ cup (80 ml) cream or
  half-and-half
1 teaspoon lemon juice
1 teaspoon chopped fresh
  tarragon leaves
Pinch cayenne pepper
Pinch salt
12 fresh oysters, shucked, or
  1 pint (450 g) shucked oysters

In a large saucepan, sauté onions and leeks in butter over medium heat until very soft, stirring frequently, about 10 minutes. Add potatoes and sauté another 5 minutes. Add chicken stock and wine and simmer until the potatoes begin to soften, about 15 to 20 minutes. Add cream or half-and-half, lemon juice, tarragon, cayenne pepper, and salt and simmer until thickened, about 5 minutes. Add oysters and their liquid and cook until the oysters are plump, no more than 5 minutes.

WINE
RECOMMENDATION:

Chardonnay
Pinot Blanc
or
Sauvignon Blanc

Potato and Bean Salad

Serves 4

8 medium red potatoes, halved
1 bay leaf
2 whole cloves garlic
4 whole peppercorns
Pinch salt

$^1/_2$ pound (225 g) fresh green beans
3 Roma tomatoes, diced
1 tablespoon red wine vinegar
2 tablespoons extra virgin olive oil
Salt and pepper to taste

To a large saucepan of boiling water, add potatoes, bay leaf, garlic, peppercorns, and salt. Boil potatoes until just about done, 13 to 18 minutes. Remove bay leaf, garlic, and peppercorns. Add beans and cook until tender, about 7 minutes. Drain, place in a bowl and toss with tomatoes. Dress lightly with vinegar and olive oil and add salt and pepper to taste.

Tomato and Sweet Onion Salad

Serves 4

1 clove garlic, mashed
2 tablespoons chopped fresh basil
$^1/_4$ teaspoon dry mustard
2 tablespoons balsamic vinegar
2 tablespoons extra virgin olive oil
Pinch sugar

Pinch salt
Freshly ground black pepper
 to taste
3 small sweet onions, peeled and
 sliced in rounds
4 medium tomatoes, cut in wedges

Mix garlic, basil, mustard, vinegar, olive oil, sugar, salt, and pepper thoroughly. Toss with onions and tomatoes. Let stand at room temperature for 30 minutes before serving.

Chilled Seafood Gazpacho
Serves 4 to 6

SOUP:

4 cups (946 ml) diced fresh
  tomatoes
1 green bell pepper, diced
1 bunch green onions, diced
1½ cups (350 ml) chicken broth
1 cup (236 ml) tomato juice or
  clam-tomato juice
2 tablespoons Sauvignon Blanc
1 can (4.5 ounce/128 g) diced
  green chilies
1 bunch green onions, chopped
2 cloves garlic, mashed
Juice of 1 lime
1 tablespoon chopped fresh
  cilantro

1 teaspoon chili powder
Salt and pepper to taste
Splash red pepper sauce

SEAFOOD:

⅓ pound (150 g) scallops, cooked
⅓ pound (150 g) crab legs, shelled
  and cooked
⅓ pound (150 g) bay shrimp,
  cooked
1 tablespoon olive oil
2 cloves garlic, mashed
Pinch salt
Juice of ½ lime

For the soup, in a blender or food processor, purée tomatoes, bell pepper, green onion, chicken broth, tomato juice, and Sauvignon Blanc until smooth. Add the remaining ingredients and mix well. Refrigerate for 1 hour.

For the seafood, mix all ingredients together and refrigerate for 1 hour. Ladle soup into individual bowls and top with seafood.

WINE
RECOMMENDATION:

*Sauvignon Blanc
or
Syrah*

37

Tuscan Bean and Bread Soup

In Tuscany, where food tends to be served simply, bean
and bread soup is just that—beans and bread in water or broth.
My version of this classic recipe utilizes other ingredients and
spices indigenous to the area to punch up the flavor.

Serves 4 to 6

1 large fennel bulb, julienned
2 yellow onions, julienned
4 cloves garlic, mashed
2 tablespoons olive oil
1 pound (450 g) dry small white
  beans or Navy beans, soaked in
  water overnight
2 quarts (1.9 l) chicken broth

1 loaf day-old French bread,
  cut into cubes and soaked in
  1 quart (946 ml) milk
Salt and pepper to taste
Truffle oil, for garnish (optional)
Parmesan cheese, for garnish
Chopped fresh Italian parsley,
  for garnish

In a 6 quart (6 l) stockpot, sauté fennel, onion, and garlic in
olive oil until very soft, about 20 minutes. Drain beans and add to
pot. Add chicken stock and simmer until beans are tender. Squeeze
out the bread and mix into the soup until blended. Season with salt
and pepper to taste. Serve in a large soup bowl and garnish with
truffle oil, Parmesan cheese, and parsley.

WINE
RECOMMENDATION:

Sauvignon Blanc

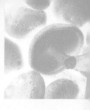

Pasta and Rice

Creamy Scallop Pasta

Serves 4

1 tablespoon butter
1 tablespoon peanut or olive oil
$^1/_2$ pound (225 g) medium bay
  scallops
2 shallots, minced
1 clove garlic, mashed
1 teaspoon chopped fresh tarragon
2 tablespoons Chardonnay

$^1/_2$ cup (118 ml) cream
Pinch lemon zest
Salt to taste
White pepper to taste
1 pound (450 g) angel hair pasta,
  cooked
Freshly grated Romano cheese,
  for garnish

In a skillet, heat butter and oil over medium heat. Add scallops and sauté briefly until lightly browned, approximately 3 minutes. Remove from pan and add shallots and garlic and sauté until soft. Add tarragon, Chardonnay, cream, lemon zest, salt, and white pepper. Simmer for 5 minutes or until slightly thickened. Return scallops to pan and simmer for a few minutes longer. Pour over cooked angel hair pasta and sprinkle with Romano cheese.

Pasta Dough

Serves 4 to 6

4 cups (450 g) unbleached all-
  purpose flour, or 2 cups semolina
  flour and 2 cups all-purpose flour

6 large eggs
Pinch salt
1 tablespoon oil

On a board, in a bowl, or in the bowl of a food processor, form a mound of flour and make a well in the center of mound. Add whole eggs and salt to the well, and mix until the flour is moistened. Mix and knead to form an elastic ball of dough, 8 to 10 minutes by hand, 2 to 3 by machine. Wrap the dough in plastic wrap and let it rest 15 to 20 minutes. Roll in a pasta machine to desired thickness (#6). Cut into strips of desired length.

WINE
RECOMMENDATION:

Chardonnay

Mediterranean Vegetarian Lasagna

Serves 4

SAUCE:

2 large onions, chopped
2 tablespoons olive oil
6 garlic cloves, chopped
1/4 cup (60 ml) chopped celery tops
4 cups (900 g) chopped Roma
 tomatoes
2 tablespoons Sauvignon Blanc
1 cup (236 ml) chicken or
 vegetable stock
2 tablespoons chopped fresh basil
2 tablespoons chopped fresh
 oregano
2 tablespoons chopped fresh
 Italian parsley
1/4 cup (57 g) chopped oil-packed
 sun-dried tomatoes

Pinch sugar
Salt and pepper to taste

LASAGNA:

6 to 8 sheets lasagna noodles
1/2 pound (225 g) portobello
 mushrooms, sliced
2 bunches fresh spinach, cleaned
 and destemmed
1/4 cup (60 g) pitted black olives,
 such as Niçoise or Kalamata
 olives
1 1/2 pounds (675 g) fresh
 mozzarella cheese, sliced
1/4 cup freshly grated
 Parmesan cheese

For the sauce, sauté onion in olive oil until soft. Add garlic and celery and sauté 3 more minutes. Add tomatoes and simmer until very soft, 10 to 15 minutes. Add Sauvignon Blanc, stock, basil, oregano, parsley, sun-dried tomatoes, and sugar. Add salt and pepper to taste. Simmer for 30 minutes. Cool.

For the lasagna, cook the pasta in boiling salted water just to al dente. Do not cook through. Rinse and sprinkle with olive oil. Preheat oven to 350°F (180°C). In a skillet, briefly sauté the mushrooms. In a large baking dish or pan, ladle a scoop of sauce onto the bottom and spread evenly. Place a layer of lasagna noodles, spread another scoop of sauce over pasta. Place 1 thin layer of spinach leaves, black olives, portobello mushroom slices, then mozzarella cheese. Add a little more sauce. Place another layer of pasta, a little sauce, and repeat the layers. Finish the top layer with pasta, sauce, and mozzarella cheese. Sprinkle with Parmesan cheese and bake for 1 hour or until sauce is bubbling and hot.

WINE
RECOMMENDATION:

*Meritage
or
Zinfandel*

Mediterranean Mussels

These mussels can also be served as an appetizer,
without the pasta.

Serves 4

2 tablespoons butter
3 shallots, finely chopped
2 cloves garlic, finely chopped
¼ cup (60 ml) Chardonnay
2 tablespoons heavy cream
1 tablespoon chopped fresh
  tarragon
½ teaspoon dry mustard

⅛ teaspoon paprika
Salt to taste
White pepper to taste
⅛ teaspoon lemon zest
1 pound (450 g) mussels,
  cleaned and debearded
1 pound (450 g) angel hair
  pasta, cooked

In a large high-sided skillet over medium heat, melt butter.
Sauté shallots and garlic until soft. Add Chardonnay and reduce by
one-third. Add cream, tarragon, dry mustard, paprika, salt, white
pepper, and lemon zest. Simmer until thickened, about 10 minutes.
Add mussels and cover. Cook until mussels are opened, about 5
minutes. Serve over cooked angel hair pasta.

WINE
RECOMMENDATION:

Chardonnay
Pinot Gris
or
Pinot Blanc

Pasta with Portobello Mushrooms and Smoked Duck Breast

Serves 4

1 large yellow onion, julienned
1 to 2 tablespoons olive oil
3 cloves garlic, mashed
1 tablespoon tomato paste
1 1/2 cups (340 g) diced tomatoes
1 cup (236 ml) veal or chicken
 stock
1/4 cup (60 ml) Sauvignon Blanc
1 cup (225 g) julienned portobello
 mushrooms

1/2 cup (113 g) julienned smoked
 duck breast
1 tablespoon chopped fresh basil
1 tablespoon chopped fresh
 Italian parsley
1/2 tablespoon chopped fresh thyme
Salt and pepper to taste
1 pound (450 g) fettuccine, cooked

In a skillet over medium heat, sauté onion and garlic in olive oil for 5 minutes. Turn heat to low and cover, simmer 15 to 20 minutes until very soft. Add tomato paste, diced tomatoes, stock, wine, mushrooms, and duck. Cover and simmer 10 minutes. Add basil, parsley, and thyme. Add salt and pepper to taste. Serve over fettuccine.

WINE
RECOMMENDATION:

*Sauvignon Blanc
or
Pinot Gris*

Pacific Rim Style Crab with Vermicelli

*I was inspired to make this dish by trips to Asia.
This flavorful, spicy offering is reminiscent of the meals
cooked in Thailand, Vietnam, and Singapore.*

Serves 4

2 cloves garlic, thinly sliced
1 tablespoon grated or thinly
  sliced fresh ginger
1 tablespoon peanut oil
$^1/_2$ teaspoon sesame oil
1 teaspoon Vietnamese fish sauce
  (optional)
1 teaspoon soy sauce or to taste
6 cups (1.4 l) chicken, vegetable,
  or seafood stock
1 pound (450 g) vermicelli or thin
  Asian rice noodles

1 tablespoon chopped
  fresh cilantro
1 tablespoon chopped fresh basil
1 tablespoon chopped fresh mint
1 bunch green onions, thinly
  sliced on diagonal
1 pound (450 g) cooked fresh
  Dungeness or king crab
Chili oil or chili paste (optional)

In a 6 quart (6 l) saucepan, over medium heat, lightly sauté the
garlic and ginger in peanut and sesame oil. Add fish sauce, soy sauce,
and stock. Bring to a low boil. Add noodles. Cook until noodles
are just tender, about 5 to 7 minutes. Stir in cilantro, basil, mint, and
green onions. Scoop into serving bowls and top with fresh crab.
Top with chili oil or paste to taste.

WINE
RECOMMENDATION:

*Sauvignon Blanc
or
Riesling*

Pacific Rim Style Crab with Vermicelli

Quick Mussel Pasta

Serves 4

1 large yellow onion, chopped
2 tablespoons olive oil
4 cloves garlic, mashed
3 cups (700 ml) chopped Roma tomatoes
2 tablespoons chopped fresh parsley
1 tablespoon chopped fresh tarragon

Juice of ¹/₂ lemon
¹/₄ cup (60 ml) Chardonnay
Salt and pepper to taste
2 pounds (900 g) fresh mussels, cleaned and debearded
12 ounces (350 g) linguini noodles, cooked
¹/₄ cup grated Parmesan cheese

In a skillet, sauté onion in olive oil until very tender. Add garlic and sauté an additional 5 minutes. Add tomatoes, cover, and cook until soft, about 10 minutes. Add parsley, tarragon, lemon juice, and Chardonnay. Add salt and pepper to taste. Sauté another 3 minutes. Add mussels and cover. Cook about 5 minutes or until mussels open. Spoon over linguini, or toss with linguini, and sprinkle with Parmesan cheese.

WINE
RECOMMENDATION:

Chardonnay

Quick Mussel Pasta

Roasted Red Pepper Sauce

This spicy pepper sauce is Croatia's answer to ketchup.
It can be used to top any pasta. I especially like it with ravioli.
It is also great as a cold spread for French bread
or as a condiment to grilled fish or chicken.

Serves 4

4 large sweet red bell peppers
1 tablespoon olive oil
2 yellow onions, thinly sliced
2 fennel bulbs, thinly sliced
4 cloves garlic, mashed

2 tablespoons olive oil
Pinch cayenne pepper
Salt to taste
1 pound (450 g) ravioli or other
    pasta, cooked

Preheat oven to 375°F (190°C). Cut peppers in half, remove seeds and stems, rub with olive oil, and bake skin-side up in the oven for 20 minutes. Remove and cool.

In a large skillet over medium-high heat, sauté onions, fennel, and garlic until soft, about 5 minutes. Lower heat to simmer, cover, and cook another 15 minutes or until very soft. Add cayenne pepper, and salt to taste. Remove from heat and cool. Add roasted peppers and blend in a food processor until smooth. Serve over hot cooked pasta.

WINE
RECOMMENDATION:

Merlot

Saifun Noodle Pasta with Scallops

Serves 4

$^{1}/_{4}$ cup (60 ml) chicken broth
2 cloves garlic, chopped
1 tablespoon grated fresh ginger
1 tablespoon peanut oil
$^{1}/_{2}$ teaspoon sesame oil
$^{1}/_{2}$ pound (225 g) bay scallops
$^{1}/_{2}$ cup (113 g) chopped
  green onions

$^{1}/_{2}$ cup (113 g) peas
1 (6 ounce/170 g) package saifun
  noodles (bean threads)
2 tablespoons Riesling
$^{1}/_{2}$ teaspoon hot pepper oil
1 teaspoon chopped fresh cilantro,
  for garnish

In a saucepan or in the microwave, bring chicken stock to a boil. In a saucepan, sauté garlic and ginger in peanut and sesame oil until soft. Add seafood and sauté quickly for 3 minutes. Add green onions and peas and remove from heat. Bring chicken stock to a boil, add noodles and Riesling and cook for 3 to 5 minutes. Bean threads cook very quickly, so be careful not to overcook. When noodles are tender, toss in scallops, green onions, and peas, and garnish with cilantro.

WINE
RECOMMENDATION:

Riesling

Potato Gnocchi

Serves 4

2 pounds (900 g) potatoes,
   peeled and halved
2 eggs
$^1/_2$ cup (113 g) ricotta cheese
$^1/_4$ cup (56 g) grated Parmesan
   cheese

Salt to taste
White pepper to taste
Pinch grated fresh nutmeg
$2^1/_2$ cups (560 g) flour
4 cups (946 ml) chicken stock

Boil potatoes until tender. Drain thoroughly. Press through ricer or mash with fork. Place potatoes on a board and make a well in the center of potatoes. Add eggs, ricotta cheese, and Parmesan cheese into the well and mix into potatoes. Add salt, white pepper, and nutmeg and mix. Continue to mix and knead, adding flour a little at a time, until forming a smooth dough. Shape into rolls approximately 1" (2.5 cm) diameter. Cut into 1" (2.5 cm) lengths and pat with fork. They should resemble little pillows. Bring chicken stock to a boil, add the gnocchi and boil until they float, about 5 minutes.

Chef's Notes:

*Gnocchi is a touchy-feely recipe and
you may need more or less flour than the
$2^1/_2$ cups. Add flour until the dough
becomes pliable and not gummy.*

WINE
RECOMMENDATION:

Sauvignon Blanc

Gnocchi with Pesto Cream Sauce

Serves 4

1 large onion, chopped
2 tablespoons butter
3 tablespoons flour
1 pint (475 ml) cream
¼ cup (60 ml) Sauvignon Blanc

Prepared pesto to taste
1 pound (450 g) gnocchi,
  or 1 recipe Potato Gnocchi
  (p. 50), cooked

In a skillet, sauté onion in butter until very soft. Sprinkle in flour. Add cream and wine. Simmer until thick. Add pesto and stir until well blended. Do not overcook. Serve with gnocchi.

Fennel and Pepper Duck with Gnocchi

Serves 4

Salt and black pepper to taste
1 duck, cut into pieces, pierce
  skin with a fork
2 tablespoons olive oil
1 large onion, thinly sliced
1 fennel bulb, julienned
1 sweet red bell pepper, julienned
2 cloves garlic, chopped
3 cups (700 ml) chopped Roma
  tomatoes
1 tablespoon chopped celery leaves

1 teaspoon chopped fresh rosemary
1 tablespoon chopped fresh parsley
⅛ teaspoon grated fresh nutmeg
1½ cups (350 ml) Merlot
1 cup (236 ml) chicken stock
Pinch sugar
1½ tablespoons tomato paste
Salt to taste
1 pound (450 kg) gnocchi, or
  1 recipe Potato Gnocchi
  (p. 50), cooked

Salt and pepper duck pieces and sauté in oil over high heat, skin-side down to render off fat, about 3 minutes. Turn and brown other side, 1 minute. Remove duck from pan and set aside. Drain off fat except for 1 tablespoon. Add onion, fennel, red pepper, and garlic to pan and sauté until soft, about 5 minutes. Add remaining sauce ingredients and bring to a boil. Add duck pieces and cover. Simmer slowly for 1 hour or until duck falls from bones. Remove bones and serve duck sauce with cooked gnocchi.

WINE
RECOMMENDATION:

Sauvignon Blanc
Merlot
or
Syrah

Stuffed Peppers

Serves 4

4 yellow or red bell peppers,
   halved lengthwise, seeded
1 pound (450 g) ground lamb
   or veal
1 large yellow onion, chopped
3 cloves garlic, mashed
2 tablespoons olive oil
2 cups (475 ml) chicken stock
$^1/_2$ cup (118 ml) Sauvignon Blanc
2 tablespoons chopped fresh
   parsley

1 cup (225 g) long grain
   white rice
2 tablespoons pine nuts
2 tablespoons golden raisins
   (sultanas)
Salt and pepper to taste
$^1/_2$ teaspoon paprika
$^1/_4$ teaspoon ground cumin
$^1/_4$ teaspoon freshly ground nutmeg

Preheat oven to 350°F (180°C). Place peppers on baking sheet or
ovenproof dish. Brown lamb, onions, and garlic in olive oil until lamb
just loses color. Add stock, wine, and parsley. Bring to a boil. Add
rice and simmer covered until rice is soft, but not competely cooked,
about 15 minutes. Remove from heat and add pine nuts, raisins,
salt and pepper, paprika, cumin, and nutmeg. Mix thoroughly. Stuff
pepper halves with the mixture. Pour just enough water around
peppers to cover bottom of the pan. Bake for 30 minutes.

WINE
RECOMMENDATION:

Merlot
or
Zinfandel

Polenta with Peas and Parmesan

Serves 4 to 6

2¹/₂ cups (590 ml) chicken stock
1 cup (225 g) fine ground cornmeal
1 cup (225 g) frozen peas, thawed

¹/₃ cup (42 g) grated Parmesan
  cheese
Salt to taste

In a deep, heavy-bottomed saucepan, bring chicken stock to a low boil. Turn to low heat, and gradually add cornmeal while stirring constantly. Stir until polenta is soft and thick, about 15 to 20 minutes. Remove from heat, and stir in thawed peas and grated Parmesan cheese. Add salt to taste.

Coconut-Curry Rice

Serves 4

1 tablespoon peanut oil
Splash chili oil
1 large onion, julienned
1 small fennel bulb, thinly sliced
1 clove garlic, mashed
¹/₂ teaspoon grated fresh ginger
2 tablespoons flour

1 cup (236 ml) chicken stock
¹/₄ cup (60 ml) coconut milk
1 teaspoon green curry paste
1 cup (225 g) jasmine or basmati
  rice, cooked according to
  package directions
Chopped fresh cilantro, for garnish

In a large skillet, add peanut and chili oils and sauté onion, fennel, garlic, and ginger over medium heat until very soft. Sprinkle with flour and continue stirring until flour has well-coated onions. Add chicken stock and stir until smooth. Add coconut milk and curry paste and simmer until thick. Pour curry sauce over rice. Garnish rice with cilantro.

Steamed Rice with Lemon Zest
Serves 4

½ teaspoon grated fresh ginger
1 garlic clove, mashed
1 tablespoon peanut oil
½ teaspoon sesame oil
Zest of ¼ lemon

2 cups (475 ml) chicken stock
Salt to taste
1 cup (225 g) uncooked
  basmati rice

In a saucepan, heat ginger and garlic in peanut and sesame oil until just soft. Add lemon zest and chicken stock and bring to a boil. Add rice and stir. Cover, turn to low, and simmer for 10 minutes. Remove cover and fluff rice. Replace cover, turn heat off and let sit for 10 minutes.

Red Beans and Rice
Serves 4

1 small onion, coarsely chopped
2 cloves garlic, minced
2 tablespoons olive oil
1 small can (3 ounces/85 g)
  chopped green chilies
1 tablespoon tomato paste
⅛ teaspoon oregano
⅛ teaspoon chili powder

Pinch cumin
½ cup (118 ml) chicken stock
1 can (15 ounce/425 g) red beans
  (substitute black beans or red
  kidney beans), drained
1½ cups (340 g) uncooked long
  grain rice

In a saucepan, sauté onions and garlic in olive oil until soft. Add green chilies, tomato paste, oregano, chili powder, cumin, and chicken stock and stir until mixed. Add drained beans, bring mixture to a simmer, and stir in rice.

Mushroom Risotto with Fresh Thyme

Serves 4

1 large onion, finely chopped
1 red bell pepper, diced
2 cloves garlic, mashed
2 tablespoons butter, divided
2 tablespoons Chardonnay
6 cups (1.4 l) chicken stock, divided
1 teaspoon chopped fresh thyme
2 cups (450 g) uncooked Arborio rice

½ pound (225 g) mixed, sliced mushrooms (chanterelle, morel, or portobello, depending on time of year)
2 rounded tablespoons mascarpone cheese
2 tablespooons milk
2 tablespoons grated Parmesan cheese
2 tablespoons chopped fresh Italian parsley

In a large saucepan, sauté onions, bell peppers and garlic in 1 tablespoon butter until quite soft. Add wine and ½ cup of chicken stock. Simmer until reduced by half. Add thyme and rice, and stir until the rice absorbs all of the liquid. Continue adding stock, 1 cup at a time, and cook until rice is al dente, stirring constantly.

Meanwhile, in a nonstick skillet, quickly sauté mushrooms in the remaining 1 tablespoon butter, until they are just lightly brown. Add mushrooms to rice, and stir in mascarpone cheese and milk. Stir until well-mixed and creamy. Garnish with Parmesan cheese and Italian parsley.

WINE
RECOMMENDATION:

Chardonnay
Sauvignon Blanc
or
Pinot Gris

Seafood Risotto

Serves 4

BASIL-ONION MIXTURE:
1/4 cup (60 g) very finely chopped
  basil leaves
3 green onions, very finely chopped
1 garlic clove, chopped
Pinch orange zest (optional)
Pinch salt
1/2 to 1 tablespoon olive oil

RISOTTO:
1 large onion, finely chopped
1 large fennel bulb, finely chopped
3 cloves garlic, chopped
2 tablespoons chopped celery
  leaves
2 tablespoons butter
2 tablespoons olive oil
2 to 3 finely chopped Roma
  tomatoes
Pinch cayenne pepper
Pinch saffron threads
1/2 cup (118 ml) Sauvignon
  Blanc
Pinch salt

2 cups (450 g) uncooked Arborio
  rice
1 quart (946 ml) chicken stock

SEAFOOD:
1 tablespoon olive oil
1 tablespoon butter
2 cloves garlic, chopped
1/3 pound (150 g) mussels, cleaned
  and debearded
1/3 pound (150 g) clams, cleaned
1/3 pound (150 g) scallops, cleaned
1/3 pound (150 g) prawns, cleaned,
  shell on
2 tablespoons Sauvignon Blanc
Juice of 1/2 lemon
1 tablespoon butter
1/3 cup (80 ml) cream
1/2 cup (113 g) frozen peas,
  thawed (optional)
2 tablespoons grated Parmesan
  cheese
Chopped fresh Italian parsley,
  for garnish

For the basil-onion mixture, in a small bowl, add the chopped basil, onions, garlic, orange zest (if using), and salt. Mix together and moisten with a small amount of olive oil. Set aside.

For the risotto, in a 6 to 8 quart (6 to 8 l) high-sided pot, sauté the onion, fennel, garlic, and celery leaves in butter and olive oil over medium heat until very wilted, about 20 minutes.

Add tomatoes. This should not look like tomato sauce but just have a whisper of tomato. Simmer until well mixed into the sauce. Add cayenne pepper, saffron, Sauvignon Blanc, and salt and simmer another 5 minutes. Add rice and stir until rice has absorbed the liquid. Add 1 cup (236 ml) of chicken stock and stir until absorbed. Continue adding chicken stock a little at a time, until all stock is absorbed and rice is tender (al dente).

For the seafood, in a sauté pan, over high heat, add olive oil and butter and sauté the garlic, mussels, clams, scallops, and prawns for 2 minutes. Add Sauvignon Blanc and lemon juice. Simmer an additional 2 minutes. Remove from heat.

Stir butter and cream into the risotto. Add peas if desired. Add the seafood with its liquid into the risotto and gently mix. Serve in bowls topped with Parmesan cheese, fresh chopped parsley, and the reserved basil-onion mixture.

WINE
RECOMMENDATION:

Chardonnay
Sauvignon Blanc
or
Pinot Gris

Sun-Dried Tomato Pasta

Serves 4

2 tablespoons olive oil
¼ pound (113 g) pancetta (Italian bacon) diced fine, or substitute American bacon
2 onions, julienned thin
3 cloves garlic, chopped
1 cup Roma tomatoes, diced
½ cup (113 g) oil-packed sun-dried tomatoes, drained and sliced
½ cup (113 g) dried porcini mushrooms, reconstituted in water, drained and sliced

2 tablespoons Chardonnay or Sauvignon Blanc
¾ cup (180 ml) chicken stock
2 tablespoons chopped fresh basil
⅓ cup (42 g) each grated Parmesan, fontina, and Romano
Salt and pepper to taste
1 tablespoon butter
1 pound (450 g) penne pasta, slightly undercooked (not quite al dente) and rinsed in cold water

Preheat oven to 325°F (160°C). Sauté pancetta in olive oil over medium heat until crispy. Add onions and garlic and cook till soft, approximately 7 to 10 minutes. Add sun-dried tomatoes, mushrooms, and chopped fresh tomatoes. Simmer for 2 minutes. Add wine and chicken stock; stir till blended and remove from heat. Stir in basil. Toss mixture with pasta. Sprinkle cheeses on pasta and toss again. Pour into a buttered casserole dish and cover with foil. Bake in oven for 15 minutes or till heated through.

Chef's Notes:

Fresh ingredients can make an incredible difference in the flavor of a dish. Avoid pre-grated Parmesan cheese. Instead buy the hard wedges of Parmesan cheese and freshly grate as much as you need for the recipe.

WINE RECOMMENDATION:

Chardonnay or Sauvignon Blanc

Seafood

Baked Salmon with Mayonnaise-Dill Sauce

*This is a good recipe for a buffet party since it can be
served warm, at room temperature, or cold.*

Serves 4 to 8

1 to 3 pound (450 g to 1.4 kg)
  side of salmon fillet
1 cup (236 ml) mayonnaise
Juice of $^1/_2$ lemon
1 tablespoon chopped fresh dill

2 cloves garlic, mashed
Dash hot pepper sauce
$^1/_2$ teaspoon white pepper
Salt to taste

    Preheat oven to 425°F (215°C). Place salmon fillet in a shallow
baking dish. Blend mayonnaise with other ingredients. Spread
evenly over salmon fillet and bake for about 20 minutes or until
fish flakes easily.

Chef's Notes:

*Dill complements salmon so well because it adds
a sharpness that cuts the richness of the salmon.*

*For an alternative to mayonnaise, try
Yogurt-Dill Sauce on page 68.*

Yogurt-Dill Sauce on page 68.

WINE
RECOMMENDATION:

*Chardonnay
or
Riesling*

Crab Cakes with Rémoulade Sauce

No crab dinner can possibly be complete without a crab cake.
This recipe is my favorite, and is accompanied
by a delicious rémoulade sauce.

Serves 4

CRAB CAKES:
1 pound (450 g) Dungeness
   crab meat
1 small red bell pepper, cored
   and diced
1 tablespoon chopped fresh
   tarragon
1 tablespoon chopped fresh
   Italian parsley
1 small yellow onion, grated
1 small Granny Smith apple,
   peeled, cored, and grated
1 teaspoon lemon juice
Dash hot pepper sauce
$^{1}/_{2}$ cup (113 g) mayonnaise
$^{1}/_{2}$ teaspoon finely ground
   white pepper

Salt to taste
1 cup (125 g) fine dry bread
   crumbs
2 tablespoons butter

RÉMOULADE SAUCE:
1 clove garlic, mashed
1 large shallot, finely chopped
1 teaspoon capers, coarsely
   chopped
1 tablespoon chopped dill pickle
Squeeze of lemon
$^{1}/_{4}$ teaspoon paprika
1 teaspoon chopped fresh tarragon
$^{1}/_{2}$ teaspoon Dijon mustard
$^{1}/_{2}$ cup (113 g) mayonnaise

For the crab cakes, in a large mixing bowl, combine crab meat,
bell pepper, tarragon, parsley, onion, apple, lemon juice, hot pepper
sauce, and mayonnaise. Add white pepper and salt to taste. Roll
and shape crab mix into $1^{1}/_{2}$" (3.8 cm) balls, flatten to $^{3}/_{4}$" (2 cm),
and lightly coat on both sides with bread crumbs. Heat a heavy
skillet to medium; add butter and sauté crab cakes on both sides
until light brown, about 3 to 5 minutes each side.

For the rémoulade sauce, mix all ingredients together until
smooth. Serve with the crab cakes.

WINE
RECOMMENDATION:

Chardonnay

Fried Oysters

Serves 4

1¹/₂ cups (170 g) fine dry bread
  crumbs
1 teaspoon paprika
Pinch chopped fresh thyme
¹/₂ teaspoon white pepper
Pinch salt
1 pint (450 g) fresh oysters,
  shucked

1 tablespoon butter
1 tablespoon olive oil
2 cloves garlic, mashed
2 tablespoons Sauvignon Blanc
1 teaspoon lemon juice

Mix bread crumbs, paprika, thyme, white pepper, and salt.
Dredge oysters in seasoned bread crumb mixture and set aside.

Heat saucepan to medium-high and add butter and olive oil.
Add garlic and sauté until light brown. Add breaded oysters and
brown on both sides, about 2 minutes each side. Remove oysters
from pan. Add wine and lemon juice to the pan and bring to a boil.
Remove from heat and pour sauce over oysters to serve.

Chef's Notes:

*In most parts of the United States, the months
ending in the letter R are best for oysters. In non-R
months, the oysters are breeding and as a result are
softer and often a bit gamey. In parts of the US
where the water is colder, as in the Pacific
Northwest, this change isn't as dramatic.
You can fry your oysters to firm them up
and thus reduce the gamey effect.*

WINE
RECOMMENDATION:

*Sauvignon Blanc
or
Pinot Gris*

Grilled Sea Bass with Cannellini Purée on a Bed of Arugula and Peppers

Serves 4

CANNELLINI PURÉE:
3 cups dried cannellini beans,
  soaked overnight then simmered
  in water until tender
1 whole bulb roasted garlic
1/8 teaspoon cumin
Salt to taste

BASIL OLIVE OIL:
1/2 cup (118 ml) firmly packed
  basil leaves
1 cup (236 ml) extra virgin
  olive oil
2 cloves garlic
Pinch salt

ARUGULA AND PEPPERS:
4 loosely packed cups fresh arugula
  or other greens
1/2 cup (113 g) sliced roasted
  red bell peppers
2 teaspoons olive oil
2 teaspoons balsamic vinegar

SEA BASS:
4 (5 ounce/150 g) sea bass fillets
2 tablespoons olive oil
Salt and pepper
Juice of 1/2 lemon

For the cannellini purée, combine all ingredients and blend until smooth.

For the arugula and peppers, toss greens with peppers, olive oil, and vinegar. Place equal portions of arugula and peppers on 4 plates. Top with bean purée.

For the basil olive oil, place all ingredients in a blender and blend until combined. Pour through fine strainer and set aside.

For the sea bass, rub olive oil, salt, and pepper over fish and grill over medium coals, 5 minutes each side. Remove the fish, sprinkle with lemon juice, and place fish on bean mixture. Drizzle basil-infused olive oil over fish before serving.

WINE
RECOMMENDATION:

Chardonnay
Pinot Gris
or
Sauvignon Blanc

Savoy Cabbage-Wrapped Salmon with Red Pepper Cream

Serves 4

SALMON:
1 clove garlic, mashed
2 tablespoons olive oil
Salt to taste
White pepper to taste
4 (4 ounce/113 g) salmon fillets
4 large savoy cabbage leaves,
  blanched and cooled
$^1/_4$ cup (60 ml) Chardonnay
Tarragon leaves, for garnish

RED PEPPER CREAM:
1 tablespoon butter
2 shallots, chopped
$^1/_8$ teaspoon lemon zest
2 tablespoons Chardonnay
1 pint heavy cream
1 red pepper, roasted, peeled and
  seeded (see Chef's Note, p. 65)
1 garlic bulb, roasted
Salt and pepper to taste

For the salmon, mix garlic, olive oil, salt, and white pepper together and rub over salmon. Wrap each fillet in a cabbage leaf. Refrigerate 30 minutes. Preheat oven to 400°F (190°C). Butter a baking dish and place salmon fillets so as not to touch. Pour Chardonnay around the fish and bake in oven for 8 to 10 minutes.

For the red pepper cream, in a saucepan, melt butter and sauté shallots in butter until soft. Add lemon zest, Chardonnay, and heavy cream. Simmer slowly until reduced by half. In a blender, purée roasted red pepper and roasted garlic. Add reduced cream mixture and blend. Put through fine sieve, if desired.

Serve the salmon wrapped in cabbage with red pepper cream. Garnish with tarragon leaves.

WINE
RECOMMENDATION:

Chardonnay

Pepper-Seared Copper River Salmon

Serves 4

2 tablespoons olive oil, divided
1 tablespoon crushed mixed
  peppercorns

¹/₄ teaspoon salt
4 (4 ounce/113 g) salmon fillets
1 tablespoon butter

Preheat oven to 375°F (190°C). Mix 1 tablespoon olive oil, pepper, and salt and rub over top of salmon fillets. In a skillet, heat the remaining olive oil and butter in sauté pan and sear salmon on top-side only until just brown. Turn over and place on a baking sheet. Bake in oven for 5 minutes.

Chef's Notes:

To roast a red bell pepper, simply preheat the oven
to 350°F (180°C), place the bell pepper in the oven
until blackened all over. When cool, slip off the skin,
and remove the stem and seeds. Alternatively, place the
pepper directly over a flame—such as a gas cooktop
or barbecue grill. Char the pepper on all sides, and
when cool, remove the skin, stem, and seeds.

WINE
RECOMMENDATION:

Chardonnay
or
Merlot

Halibut Roast with Soy-Ginger Baste

Serves 4

1 (2 to 3 pound/1 to 1.4 kg)
  whole halibut roast
  (end piece skin on)
¹/₂ tablespoon peanut oil
¹/₂ teaspoon sesame oil
¹/₂ teaspoon pepper oil
1" (2.5 cm) piece fresh ginger,
  thinly sliced
2 cloves garlic, thinly sliced

¹/₄ cup (60 ml) soy sauce
2 tablespoons Riesling or
  Sauvignon Blanc
Squeeze of lemon
1 teaspoon honey
2 tablespoons chopped
  fresh cilantro
1 bunch green onions, cut lengthwise into long strips, for garnish

Preheat oven to 375°F (190°C). Place halibut in shallow roasting pan. In a small saucepan, mix peanut oil, sesame oil, and pepper oil over medium-high heat. Add the ginger and garlic and sauté until just tender, not brown. Add soy sauce, wine, lemon juice, and honey and simmer for 5 minutes. Brush halibut generously with soy mixture and bake covered for 10 minutes. Remove cover and baste again with remaining soy mixture. Bake another 10 to 15 minutes or until fish flakes easily. Garnish with green onions.

Chef's Notes:

Baked or grilled halibut wouldn't normally match
well with red wine, but the soy-gingery flavor
of this baste goes beautifully with Merlot and Syrah.
If you'd like to use a white wine instead,
Sauvignon Blanc will work well in this dish.

WINE
RECOMMENDATION:

Sauvignon Blanc
Merlot
or
Syrah

Grilled Marinated Northwest King Salmon

Serves 4

4 (6 ounce/170 g) salmon fillets, cut on bias
1/4 cup (60 ml) Chardonnay
1 tablespoon chopped fresh parsley
2 teaspoons chopped fresh tarragon
2 tablespoons olive oil
1 large clove garlic, mashed
1/8 teaspoon paprika
Juice of 1/2 lemon
Salt to taste
White pepper to taste
Mixed greens, for serving

Mix ingredients and marinate salmon for 1 hour. Preheat barbecue. Grill over hot coals about 5 to 7 minutes each side, until opaque throughout. Place salmon on a bed of greens.

Halibut in Foil

Serves 4

1 1/2 pounds (675 g) halibut fillet
1 tomato, thinly sliced
2 cloves garlic, mashed
2 tablespoons chopped fresh basil
1 tablespoon balsamic vinegar
2 tablespoons extra virgin olive oil
2 tablespoons Sauvignon Blanc
1/2 teaspoon dry mustard
Salt and pepper to taste

Make a "boat" out of aluminum foil, and place fish in the foil. Top with sliced tomatoes, garlic, and basil. In a separate bowl, mix vinegar, oil, wine, and dry mustard. Add salt and pepper to taste. Pour over fish. Grill fish over medium hot coals until fish flakes easily, about 15 minutes.

WINE RECOMMENDATION:

Chardonnay

Scrambled Eggs with Smoked Salmon and Dill

Serves 4

6 eggs
2 tablespoons sour cream, plus
  additional for garnish
$^1/_3$ cup (75 g) sliced smoked
  salmon
1 tablespoon chopped fresh dill
Splash hot pepper sauce

Salt to taste
White pepper to taste
1 tablespoon butter
2 English muffins, halved
  and toasted
4 dill sprigs, for garnish

In a medium bowl, beat eggs. Mix in sour cream, smoked salmon, fresh dill, and hot pepper sauce. Add salt and white pepper to taste. In a hot skillet, melt butter. Cook the egg mixture, stirring occasionally until done. Eggs should be moist.

Place equal amounts of egg on each of the 4 English muffin halves. Dot with sour cream and garnish with dill sprig.

Yogurt-Dill Sauce

Use this delicious sauce as a condiment for salmon instead of mayonnaise. Once you've tried it, you may find yourself using it as a condiment to grilled hamburgers or ground lamb patties as well.

1 pint (450 g) plain yogurt
2 cloves garlic, mashed
2 tablespoons lemon juice
Pinch sugar
1 teaspoon dry mustard

2 tablespoons chopped fresh dill
Salt to taste
White pepper to taste
Splash hot pepper sauce

Combine all ingredients and blend well.

Seared Halibut with Mediterranean Couscous

Serves 4

COUSCOUS:
2 cups (475 ml) chicken broth
2 cups (475 ml) water
2 cups (475 ml) couscous

FISH:
4 (6 ounce/180 g) halibut fillets, skin off
2 tablespoons olive oil
1/2 cup (118 ml) Sauvignon Blanc

TOMATO MIXTURE:
2 cups (475 ml) chopped Roma tomatoes
6 green onions, chopped
1 tablespoon capers
2 tablespoons pitted, chopped Kalamata olives
4 anchovy fillets, chopped
2 tablespoons chopped fresh basil
2 tablespoons chopped fresh Italian parsley
Pinch ground cumin
Pinch red pepper flakes
2 to 3 tablespoons balsamic vinegar
2 tablespoons extra virgin olive oil

Preheat oven to 350°F (180°C).

For the couscous, in a 4 quart (4 l) saucepan, bring chicken broth and water to a boil. Add couscous and cook as you would pasta, until just al dente.

For the fish, in a hot skillet, add olive oil and sear halibut fillets on one side only, for about 2 minutes. Remove and turn over onto a flat baking dish. Pour Sauvignon Blanc around fish and bake for about 6 minutes.

Mix together tomatoes, green onions, capers, olives, anchovies, basil, parsley, cumin, and pepper flakes and toss with balsamic vinegar and olive oil. When couscous is done, gently mix with the tomato mixture and place on 4 plates. Top with halibut fillet.

WINE RECOMMENDATION:

Syrah
or
Sauvignon Blanc

Grilled Black Cod

Serves 4

1 tablespoon peanut oil
$1/4$ teaspoon sesame oil
1 teaspoon thinly sliced fresh
  ginger
2 cloves garlic, mashed
3 green onions, chopped
Splash Dry Riesling or
  Sauvignon Blanc

2 tablespoons rice vinegar
1 tablespoon lightly crushed
  fermented black beans
1 tablespoon chopped fresh
  cilantro
Juice of $1/2$ lime
2 pounds (900 g) black cod fillet

Preheat barbecue grill. In a saucepan, heat peanut oil and sesame oil. Add ginger and garlic and sauté until tender, 2 to 3 minutes. Add remaining ingredients, except cod, and simmer for 3 minutes. Over medium coals, cook black cod, skin-side down, basting with the sauce, for 7 to 10 minutes or until it flakes. Transfer fish to a platter and pour sauce over fish.

Chef's Notes:

*When looking for fermented black beans,
be sure to get the dry variety, not the black bean
paste. The paste contains overpowering
amounts of garlic and oil.*

WINE
RECOMMENDATION:

*Sauvignon Blanc
or
Riesling*

Spicy Sautéed Prawns

Serves 4 to 6

1 pound (450 kg) prawns, peeled
  and deveined
1 tablespoon peanut oil (optional)

Sauce:
1 tablespoon peanut oil
1 teaspoon sesame oil
1 tablespoon soy sauce
1 tablespoon Vietnamese fish sauce

¼ teaspoon crushed red pepper
  paste
2 tablespoons Sauvignon Blanc
1 teaspoon lime juice
3 garlic cloves, mashed
½ teaspoon grated fresh ginger
1 tablespoon chopped fresh
  cilantro

Preheat barbecue grill. Thread prawns on metal skewers or
bamboo skewers that have been soaked for 30 minutes in water. Mix
sauce ingredients together. Baste prawns with sauce and grill on both
sides until just beginning to change color.

Alternatively, in a large skillet over medium-high heat, sauté
prawns in peanut oil just until they begin to change color. Add the
sauce and continue to cook another 5 minutes.

Steamed Mussels

Serves 4 to 6

2 pounds (900 g) mussels, cleaned
  and debearded
½ cup (113 g) diced tomatoes
3 cloves garlic, mashed
6 green onions, chopped
1 tablespoon olive oil

Juice of ½ lemon
2 tablespoons Sauvignon Blanc
2 tablespoons chopped fresh
  cilantro
2 tablespoons chopped fresh basil
Pinch red pepper flakes

Combine all ingredients in a large pot with a lid. Cover and
steam on high heat, skaking the pot vigorously every couple of
minutes during steaming, for about 8 minutes or until
mussels open.

Wine
Recommendation:

*Dry Riesling
or
Sauvignon Blanc*

Sweet and Sour Marlin

Serves 4

$^1/_3$ cup (80 ml) soy sauce
$^1/_2$ teaspoon grated fresh ginger
2 cloves garlic, mashed
$^1/_3$ cup (80 ml) chicken stock
$^1/_2$ teaspoon sesame oil
1 teaspoon peanut oil
1 tablespoon orange marmalade
$^1/_4$ cup (60 ml) Riesling

Juice of 1 lime
Pinch red pepper flakes
1 tablespoon chopped fresh
  cilantro
1 tablespoon rice vinegar
1 teaspoon honey
4 (5 ounce/150 g) marlin fillets
  or ahi fillets

In a medium saucepan, combine all ingredients except fish. Simmer until reduced by at least half. Cool sauce. Preheat barbecue grill. Generously baste fish with sauce. Grill fish over hot coals, basting often, for 5 minutes each side.

Hot Pepper-Cilantro Pesto

Use on grilled ahi or Chicken Skewers (p. 90-91).

Serves 4

$^1/_2$ cup (118 ml) chopped fresh
  cilantro leaves
4 green onions, chopped
1 clove garlic, chopped
$^1/_2$ teaspoon grated fresh ginger

2 jalapeño peppers, chopped
1 to 2 tablespoons peanut oil
$^1/_4$ teaspoon sesame oil
Squeeze of lime
Salt to taste

In a blender, combine all ingredients until smooth.

WINE
RECOMMENDATION:

*Johannisberg
Riesling
or
Merlot*

Baked Cod with Tomato Concassé and Basil

This is one of my favorite fish recipes.
Halibut or sea bass could be substituted.

Serves 4 to 6

²/₃ cup (85 g) fine bread crumbs
¹/₃ cup (42 g) grated Parmesan
  cheese
¹/₄ teaspoon dry thyme
¹/₃ cup (80 ml) extra virgin olive
  oil, divided
3 garlic cloves, thinly sliced
2 shallots, thinly sliced

1 to 1¹/₂ pounds (450 to 675 g)
  true cod or black cod fillet
Juice of ¹/₂ lemon
3 Roma tomatoes, finely chopped
¹/₂ cup (118 ml) Sauvignon Blanc
2 tablespoons chopped fresh basil

Preheat oven to 450°F (230°C). Mix bread crumbs, cheese, and thyme together and set aside. In a skillet, heat 1 tablespoon olive oil, slowly cook garlic and shallots until very soft, 7 to 10 minutes. Remove and cool slightly. Pour 2 tablespoons of olive oil into the bread mixture and mix. Bread crumbs should be moist, not wet. Spread the mixture evenly over the fish. Sprinkle with lemon juice. In a large baking dish pour the remaining olive oil with garlic and shallots evenly on the bottom of the dish. Lay fish fillet on the oil and sprinkle tomatoes around the fillets. Pour wine over tomatoes (not fish). Bake in oven until bread crumbs and cheese have browned slightly. Remove fillet and mix the remaining juices and tomatoes with basil and spoon over fish.

WINE
RECOMMENDATION:

Sauvignon Blanc
or
Pinot Gris

Curried Shrimp

Serves 4 to 6

1 pound (450 g) large shrimp,
  peeled and deveined
1 yellow onion, finely chopped
2 cloves garlic, finely chopped
¹/₂ teaspoon grated fresh ginger
1 tablespoon butter
1 tablespoon peanut oil
1¹/₂ tablespoons flour

1 tablespoon lemon juice
2 tablespoons Sauvignon Blanc
¹/₂ cup (118 ml) fish stock
¹/₂ cup (118 ml) cream or
  half-and-half
¹/₂ teaspoon Madras curry powder
Salt to taste

In a skillet, sauté shrimp, onion, garlic, and ginger in butter and peanut oil until just tender, 3 to 5 minutes. Sprinkle with flour to coat shrimp. Add lemon juice, wine, fish stock, cream, curry powder, and salt. Simmer until thickened, about 3 minutes.

Chef's Notes:

*The easiest way to make a delicious fish stock
is to simmer 2 cups (450 g) of shrimp or prawn shells
in a saucepan with ¹/₂ (118 ml) cup dry white wine
and ¹/₂ (118 ml) cup water. Let simmer for
15 minutes and strain the stock.*

WINE
RECOMMENDATION:

*Riesling
or
Sauvignon Blanc*

Poultry

Chicken and Three Pepper Fajitas

Serves 4

2 whole boneless chicken breasts
1 red bell pepper, julienned
1 yellow bell pepper, julienned
1 green bell pepper, julienned
1 large sweet onion, sliced
2 cloves garlic, mashed
2 tablespoons olive oil
2 tablespoons Chardonnay

Juice of ½ lemon
1 tablespoon chili powder
Pinch red pepper flakes
2 tablespoons chopped fresh
  cilantro
Salt to taste
4 fresh corn tortillas
1 head lettuce, shredded

Slice chicken breasts into strips and set aside. In a large skillet, sauté peppers, onions, and garlic in oil until soft. Add chicken breasts and sauté quickly. Add remaining ingredients, stir well, and cook over medium-high heat. Remove from heat. Using a slotted spoon, spread onto tortillas and top with shredded lettuce.

Chicken Fricassee

Serves 4

1 (3 to 5 pound/1.3 to 2.3 kg)
  broiler-fryer chicken,
  cut into pieces
Flour, for dusting
2 tablespoons olive oil
1½ cups (350 ml) onion,
  thinly sliced
4 cloves garlic, chopped
2 cups (475 ml) chopped Roma
  tomatoes

2 tablespoons chopped celery tops
2 tablespoons chopped celery
1 tablespoon chopped fresh basil
1 tablespoon chopped fresh
  rosemary
1 tablespoon lemon juice
¼ cup (30 ml) Sauvignon Blanc
¼ cup (57 g) frozen dark
  sweet cherries
Pinch red pepper flakes to taste

Lightly flour chicken pieces and brown on both sides in olive oil, about 7 minutes each side. Remove chicken from pan and add onion and garlic. Sauté until very tender. Add remaining ingredients. Return chicken to the sauce and cook for 20 to 30 minutes, covered.

WINE
RECOMMENDATION:

Sauvignon Blanc
Zinfandel
or
Merlot

Chicken and Zinfandel

Serves 4

1 (3 to 5 pound/1.3 to 2.3 kg)
  broiler-fryer chicken,
  cut into 8 pieces
Salt and black pepper to taste
2 tablespoons olive oil
1 yellow onion, julienned
3 cloves garlic, mashed
1 tablespoon tomato paste
1/2 cup (118 ml) chopped tomatoes

1 cup (236 ml) Zinfandel
2 whole sprigs fresh rosemary
Pinch grated fresh nutmeg
1 whole clove
1 bay leaf
2 tablespoons chopped fresh
  Italian parsley, for garnish
2 tablespoons grated fresh
  Parmesan cheese, for garnish

In a high-sided skillet, sprinkle chicken with salt and pepper and brown chicken pieces in olive oil. Remove browned chicken. Add onion and garlic to the skillet and sauté for 5 minutes. Stir in tomato paste. Add tomatoes, wine, rosemary, clove, and bay leaf and bring to a boil. Return chicken to pan and reduce heat to a simmer. Cook covered for 30 minutes, turning chicken occasionally. Remove cover and simmer another 5 minutes to reduce sauce. Garnish with parsley and Parmesan cheese.

Chef's Notes:

Guiseppi, the father of my dear friend
Joe Tranquilli, used to cook chicken in his
homemade Zinfandel with a recipe much like this
from his home town of Porto St. Giorgeo on
the Italian Adriatic. This dish should be a little
on the dry side, in other words, not too saucy.

WINE
RECOMMENDATION:

Zinfandel

Chicken Breasts with Champagne and Mushrooms

Serves 4

2 boneless chicken breasts, halved
1 tablespoon butter
1 tablespoon olive oil
2 cloves garlic, mashed
1 small onion, julienned
1 cup (236 ml) sliced fresh
 mushrooms (chanterelles,
 button, or other seasonal
 fresh mushrooms)

¹/₄ cup (60 ml) sparkling wine
¹/₂ cup (118 ml) chicken broth
1 teaspoon dry mustard
1 teaspoon chopped fresh
 Italian parsley
1 teaspoon chopped fresh thyme
Salt and pepper to taste

In a large skillet, add chicken pieces to heated butter and oil and brown over medium-high heat until brown on both sides, about 5 minutes each side. Remove chicken and place on warming plate or in 200°F (95°C) oven. In the skillet used to cook the chicken pieces, add garlic, onions, and mushrooms and brown for 3 minutes. Add wine, chicken broth, mustard, parsley, thyme, and salt and pepper and simmer for 5 to 10 minutes or until liquid is reduced by half. Pour over chicken breasts and serve.

Chef's Notes:

Even though the bubbles in champagne dissipate when it's cooked, there is still a special, festive taste that results from using sparkling wine in a dish. For a gala meal, go against convention and serve champagne along with this entrée.

WINE
RECOMMENDATION:

Sparkling Wine

Chicken Paprika
Serves 4

1 (3 to 5 pound/1.3 to 2.3 kg)
  broiler-fryer chicken,
  cut into 6 pieces
Flour, for dredging
1 tablespoon olive oil
1 tablespoon butter
3 cloves garlic, mashed
2 medium onions, thinly sliced

1 cup (236 ml) chicken stock
2 tablespoons Sauvignon Blanc
1 teaspoon paprika
1 tablespoon flour mixed with
  water to form a thin paste
Salt and pepper to taste
$^1\!/_2$ cup (118 ml) sour cream

Dredge chicken pieces in flour. In a large covered skillet, add olive oil and butter. Over medium heat, brown chicken on both sides. Remove from pan. Add garlic and onions and sauté until soft. Return chicken to pan. Add chicken stock and wine. Cover and simmer for 1 hour. When chicken is tender, mix paprika into flour and water and add to pan. Stir into sauce and simmer an additional 10 minutes. Turn heat to low and stir in sour cream before serving.

Roast Capon
Serves 4

1 (3 to 5 pound/1.3 to 2.3 kg)
  capon
2 tablespoons peanut oil
1 tablespoon sesame oil
1 teaspoon freshly grated ginger

4 cloves garlic, mashed
Juice of 1 lemon
2 tablespoons Dry Riesling
1 tablespoon soy sauce
$^1\!/_2$ teaspoon dry mustard

Preheat oven to 325°F (160°C). Place capon in a baking dish. Combine all remaining ingredients together in a bowl and mix well. Brush capon with basting sauce. Place capon in oven and cook for $1^1\!/_2$ hours, basting frequently with sauce.

WINE
RECOMMENDATION:

Sauvignon Blanc

Croatian Chicken

This is a very traditional Dalmatian Coast way
of "baking" chicken—moist and flavorful.

Serves 4

1 (3 to 5 pound/1.3 to 2.3 kg)
  broiler-fryer chicken,
  cut into 8 pieces
Salt and freshly ground black
  pepper
2 tablespoons olive oil
1 large yellow onion, julienned
1 red bell pepper, julienned
1 yellow bell pepper, julienned
1 fennel bulb, julienned
6 cloves garlic, chopped

1 tablespoon chopped fresh
  Italian parsley
1 tablespoon chopped fresh
  rosemary
Pinch red pepper flakes
¼ teaspoon dry mustard
¼ cup (60 ml) Sauvignon Blanc
½ (10.5 ounces/300 g) can
  chicken broth or homemade
  stock

Preheat oven to 350°F (180°C). Sprinkle chicken pieces with
salt and pepper. In a large skillet with lid, brown chicken in olive oil
for about 5 to 7 minutes each side. Transfer chicken to a high-sided
baking pan. In the skillet used to cook chicken, sauté onion, red
pepper, yellow pepper, fennel, and garlic over medium-high heat
until soft, about 5 to 10 minutes. Remove from heat. Add parsley,
rosemary, pepper flakes, dry mustard, wine, and chicken broth.
Season with salt and pepper to taste. Pour around chicken pieces.
Bake for 30 minutes. Turn chicken and stir vegetables. Cook an
additional 30 minutes.

WINE
RECOMMENDATION:

Sauvignon Blanc

Roasted Chicken

My grandmother used a traditional method in preparing fresh poultry for cooking. Before cooking, she would soak the entire bird for an hour in a large pot with ice cold, highly salted water.

Serves 6

BASTING SAUCE:
2 tablespoons olive oil
Juice of 1 lemon
2 tablespoons Chardonnay
3 cloves garlic, mashed
1 tablespoon fresh chopped parsley
1 tablespoon fresh chopped oregano

1 tablespoon fresh chopped rosemary
$^1/_4$ teaspoon cumin
$^1/_4$ teaspoon paprika
$^1/_2$ teaspoon dry mustard
Salt and pepper to taste
1 whole (3 to 5 pound/1.3 to 2.3 kg) roasting chicken

Preheat oven to 350°F (180°C). In a small bowl, mix together all ingredients. Wash chicken and pat dry, inside and out. Invert wings so top of wings are under body and tie legs together with kitchen twine. To get a nice and even roast, cook on a rack so it is held above the pan. Put chicken in oven for 5 minutes without basting sauce. This will dry out the skin, so that you can then baste chicken. Baste and return chicken to oven, and continue to baste every 15 to 20 minutes for 1 hour, depending on size. An easy way to tell if a chicken is done, is to grab the drumstick and wiggle; if it's loose, it's done.

Another, quicker, way to "roast" chicken is to: Cut chicken in half, or buy a split broiler. Put on baking pan or cookie sheet, skin-side down. Baste ahead of time, slathering baste over all halves, for 10 to 15 minutes. If you can do so, set broiler to medium. If not, put rack on second highest position. Put chicken under broiler skin-side down, until just brown. Baste again. Flip chicken over and cook until skin just browns, about 3 to 4 minutes. Move chicken from broiler, and move rack to middle position. Change oven setting to bake at 325°F (160°C), and put chicken back in oven for another 15 minutes. The finished product is a fully cooked chicken that is half broiled but still has roasted chicken flavor.

WINE
RECOMMENDATION:

Sauvignon Blanc

Spicy Southwest-Style Chicken Barbecue

Serves 4

1 (3 to 5 pound/1.3 to 2.3 kg)
broiler-fryer chicken, cut into
pieces
2 tablespoons olive oil
Juice of 1 lemon
Juice of 1 lime
2 tablespoons Sauvignon Blanc
4 cloves garlic
1 small can (4 ounces/113 g)
chopped green chilies
6 green onions, chopped

2 tablespoons chopped fresh
cilantro
2 tablespoons chopped fresh
parsley
$^1/_2$ teaspoon chopped fresh
oregano
1 teaspoon chili powder
2 tablespoons tomato paste
Salt and pepper to taste
Hot pepper sauce to taste
(optional)

Preheat grill, or oven to 350°F (180°C). Place chicken
in large baking dish. In a food processor, combine all remaining
ingredients. Mix thoroughly but do not overblend. Marinate chicken
in mixture for 1 hour in refrigerator. Barbecue chicken on grill,
7 to 10 minutes each side until cooked or bake in oven for 1$^1/_2$ hours,
basting frequently with marinade.

WINE
RECOMMENDATION:

*Sauvignon Blanc
or
Zinfandel*

Chicken Breasts with Sun-Dried Tomato Crème

Serves 4

2 boneless chicken breasts, halved
2 tablespoons butter
2 shallots, chopped
1 clove garlic, chopped
1/4 cup (60 ml) Sauvignon Blanc
1/8 teaspoon lemon zest
1/2 cup (118 ml) whipping cream

2 tablespoons chopped oil-packed sun-dried tomatoes
Salt to taste
White pepper to taste
1 teaspoon chopped fresh tarragon
1 tablespoon chopped fresh basil

In a large skillet, heat butter and sauté chicken breasts over medium-high heat, about 5 minutes each side, until brown on both sides. Remove chicken and keep warm. In same pan, add shallots and garlic. Sauté 2 minutes. Add wine and lemon zest and let simmer for 3 to 5 minutes. Add cream and sun-dried tomatoes. Add salt, white pepper, tarragon, and basil and reduce by one-third or until thick.

Slice chicken breasts on an angle and place on a pool of Sun-Dried Tomato Crème.

WINE RECOMMENDATION:

Dry Riesling
or
Sauvignon Blanc

Szechuan Chicken

Serves 4

4 boneless, skinless chicken breasts

MARINADE:
2 green minced onions
2 tablespoons fresh minced cilantro
1 tablespoon minced garlic
1 tablespoon minced ginger
3 tablespoons dry sherry

2 tablespoons hoisin sauce
3 tablespoons soy sauce
$1^1/_2$ tablespoons red wine vinegar
1 tablespoon dark soy sauce
1 tablespoon sesame oil
1 teaspoon sugar
1 teaspoon Chinese chili sauce
  or other hot chili sauce

Combine all marinade ingredients together. Marinate chicken
for 2 hours in refrigerator. Preheat oven to 350°F (180°C) or heat
barbecue. Bake in oven or grill over medium coals, basting frequently,
until juices run clear, about 20 to 25 minutes if in the oven, or 5 to 8
minutes each side, on the grill.

Meats

Beef and Cabernet

Serves 4

1¹/₂ to 2 pounds (675 to 900 g)
 beef chuck roast, cut into
 1¹/₂" (4 cm) pieces
Flour, for dredging
2 tablespoons olive oil
1 yellow onion, finely chopped
1 red bell pepper, diced
1 yellow bell pepper, diced
2 garlic cloves, chopped
1 cup (225 g) chopped Roma
 tomatoes

1 tablespoon tomato paste
1 cup (236 ml) beef stock
1 cup (236 ml) Cabernet
 Sauvignon
1 bouquet garni of thyme,
 rosemary and bay leaf,
 tied with twine
1 teaspoon dry mustard
Salt and pepper to taste
¹/₃ pound (150 g) small
 boiling onions, peeled

Preheat oven to 350°F (180°C). Dredge beef in flour. In Dutch oven or large covered ovenproof pot, brown beef in olive oil on all sides, and remove. Add onions, peppers, garlic, and tomatoes, and sauté until soft. Add tomato paste and simmer 5 minutes. Add beef stock, Cabernet Sauvignon, bouquet garni, and dry mustard. Add salt and pepper to taste. Bring to a simmer and cook 10 minutes. Return meat to the pot, add the boiling onions and cover.

Bake in oven for 1¹/₂ hours, stirring occasionally, until meat is very tender.

WINE
RECOMMENDATION:

*Cabernet
Sauvignon*

Braised Veal Roast

*This is best served over wide noodles,
like fettucine or pappardelle.*

Serves 4 to 6

1 to 3 pound (450 g to 1.35 kg)
  veal roast (chuck or shoulder)
Flour, for dredging
1 tablespoon olive oil
1 large yellow onion, finely
  julienned
1 large red bell pepper, finely
  julienned
3 cloves garlic, chopped
1 bay leaf

$^1/_8$ teaspoon paprika
1 tablespoon chopped fresh Italian
  parsley, plus extra for garnish
1 teaspoon chopped fresh thyme
Grated fresh nutmeg to taste
1" (2.5 cm) thin strip orange zest
$^1/_2$ cup (118 ml) Sauvignon Blanc
1 cup (236 ml) chicken or
  veal stock
Salt to taste

Preheat oven to 325°F (160°C). Dredge veal roast in flour. In a
large Dutch oven or pot, brown veal roast in oil on all sides. Remove
from pot. Add onion, bell pepper, and garlic and sauté until soft. Add
bay leaf, paprika, parsley, thyme, nutmeg, orange zest, Sauvignon
Blanc, and veal stock. Add salt to taste. Bring to a simmer and add
roast back to pot. Cover and cook in oven for 30 minutes. Turn roast
over and cook for another 30 minutes or until meat is fork tender
and temperature on meat thermometer registers 170°F (77°C).
Garnish with chopped Italian parsley.

WINE
RECOMMENDATION:

*Syrah
or
Merlot*

Brine-Soaked Pork Loin

Serve this with Red Beans and Rice, page 54.

Serves 4

BRINE MIXTURE:
4 quarts (3.8 l) water
2 onions, chopped
4 garlic cloves, chopped
2 bay leaves
$^1/_2$ teaspoon cumin seeds
$^1/_2$ teaspoon fennel seeds
$^1/_2$ teaspoon thyme
$^1/_2$ teaspoon whole peppercorns
$^1/_2$ cup (113 g) salt

1 cup (236 ml) Sauvignon Blanc
2 or 3 sprigs parsley
2 sprigs rosemary

PORK LOIN:
1 to 3 pound (450 g to 1.35 kg)
   pork loin
1 tablespoon olive oil
Generous amount fresh cracked
   pepper

For the brine, begin preparing 1 day before serving. Mix all brine ingredients together in a 6 quart (6 l) saucepan and bring to a boil. Reduce to a simmer and cook uncovered for 30 minutes. Remove from heat and cool. For the pork, add pork loin to the brine mixture and refrigerate overnight.

Preheat barbecue grill. Remove pork from brine. Rub with olive oil and fresh cracked pepper. Barbecue over medium coals, covered, for 15 minutes. Turn roast, and cook another 15 minutes. Pork is done when temperature reaches 180°F (90°C).

Chef's Notes:

Once this dish is cooked, the pork roast has a reddish outer skin. This is normal in brining, almost a "smoked" look. Some chefs have used whole chickens and rave about the results.

WINE
RECOMMENDATION:

*Sauvignon Blanc
or
Cabernet
Sauvignon*

Herb-Rubbed Rib Roast

Serves 8

1 (8 to 10 pound/3.6 to 4.5 kg)
  standing rib roast, bone in
3 cloves garlic, thinly sliced

MARINADE:
4 tablespoons olive oil
2 tablespoons Cabernet Sauvignon
3 cloves garlic, finely chopped
1 tablespoon chopped fresh thyme

1 tablespoon chopped fresh
  rosemary
1 tablespoon chopped fresh Italian
  parsley
$^1/_2$ tablespoon dry mustard
1 teaspoon Worcestershire sauce
Salt and pepper to taste
Grated fresh horseradish

Make an incision every 2" (5 cm) on the roast and insert slices
of garlic. Mix together all marinade ingredients and rub over the
roast. Let roast stand for 1 hour at room temperature.

Preheat oven to 350°F (180°C). Bake roast in oven for 2 hours
(or 20 minutes per pound) for medium-rare, or until temperature
on meat thermometer registers 150°F (66°C). Serve with horseradish.

Kobe-Style Ribs

Serves 4

2 pounds (900 g) Kobe-style short
  ribs (thinly-cut beef short ribs)
1 tablespoon peanut oil
$^1/_4$ teaspoon sesame oil
$^1/_4$ teaspoon ground cloves
3 cloves garlic, mashed
$^1/_2$ tablespoon grated fresh ginger

1 tablespoon honey
1 tablespoon tomato paste
2 to 3 tablespoons soy sauce
2 tablespoons Cabernet-Merlot
$^1/_2$ teaspoon dry mustard
2 tablespoons chopped fresh
  cilantro (optional)

Combine all ingredients, except short ribs. Pour mixture
over ribs and marinate overnight or at least 1 hour. Excellent
grilled on the barbecue, 7 minutes each side. Ribs can
also be placed in a baking pan and baked in the oven
at 350°F (180°C) until tender, about 2 hours.

WINE
RECOMMENDATION:

*Merlot
or
Cabernet
Sauvignon*

Mixed Skewers

Serves 4

MARINADE:

1 tablespoon chopped fresh
oregano

1 cup extra virgin olive oil

$^1/_3$ cup (80 ml) Sauvignon Blanc
or Pinot Gris

4 cloves garlic, mashed

2 tablespoons chopped fresh Italian
parsley

1 tablespoon chopped fresh
oregano

$^1/_2$ teaspoon cumin

Pinch crushed red pepper flakes

Juice of 1 lemon

1 teaspoon dry mustard

Salt and white pepper to taste

SKEWERS:

Choose from chicken and sausage,
vegetable or seafood (p. 91)

For the marinade, place all marinade ingredients in a blender
or food processor, and blend thoroughly; mixture will be quite thick.

Preheat barbecue grill or broiler 15 minutes before barbecuing.
Put all skewers on a large baking sheet, and baste with marinade.
Over medium heat, or when charcoal has gone white, barbecue all
skewers for 4 minutes. Turn and baste, cook for 4 minutes, then turn
and baste again. Because of the consistent size of the skewer cubes,
all of these skewers should cook at the same rate. When prawns turn
an orange-white color, and when vegetables begin to become tender
to the touch, the skewers are done.

WINE
RECOMMENDATION:

*Pinot Gris
or
Sauvignon Blanc*

Meats

CHICKEN AND SAUSAGE SKEWERS:

4 Italian sausages (pork or chicken)   2 boneless chicken breasts
4 boneless chicken thighs   1 large red onion, quartered

    Cut each sausage into three equal pieces. Cut chicken breasts and thighs into 1" (2.5 cm) cubes. Pierce meat and onion onto a bamboo or metal skewer, alternating meat layers with onion layers until at least 4 skewers are full.

VEGETABLE SKEWERS:

1 eggplant, cut into   2 yellow peppers, cut into
  1" (2.5 cm) cubes   1" (2.5 cm) cubes
2 portobello mushrooms,   6 baby zucchini, cut into rings
  cut into 1" (2.5 cm) cubes   2 yellow onions, quartered
2 red peppers, cut into
  1" (2.5 cm) cubes

    Pierce vegetables onto bamboo or metal skewer, placing zucchini, as the hardest vegetable, on bottom. Continue alternating vegetables as you please, or onion, eggplant, onion, mushroom, zucchini, until 4 skewers are full.

SEAFOOD SKEWERS:

1 pound (450 g), or 16 to 20 $^1/_2$ pound (225 g) firm cherry
  prawns, peeled and deveined   tomatoes
3 tuna steaks, about 1" (2.5 cm) 1 bunch basil leaves
  thick, cut into 1" (2.5 cm) cubes

    Pierce seafood and tomatoes onto a bamboo or metal skewer, beginning with a prawn, and followed by basil leaf, tomato, tuna, basil leaf, and another prawn until 4 skewers are full.

Panini

This is my best friend, Frank Algiere's, favorite food,
the panini, which means "little sandwich" in Italian.
His is cold, mine is grilled.

Serves 4

1 loaf ciabatta, foccacia, or
  baguette style bread, halved
  lengthwise
$^1/_2$ cup (118 ml) extra virgin
  olive oil
1 clove garlic, mashed
1 tablespoon chopped fresh
  Italian parsley
1 tablespoon chopped fresh basil

Pinch salt
$^1/_4$ pound (113 g) sliced prosciutto
$^1/_4$ pound (113 g) sliced fontina
  cheese
$^1/_4$ cup (60 ml) sliced roasted
  red peppers
$^1/_2$ cup (118 ml) fresh arugula
  (rocket) leaves or spinach

Mix the oil, garlic, parsley, basil, and salt together and brush both cut sides of the bread with the mixture.

On one side of the bread layer the prosciutto, cheese, peppers, and arugula. Put the other half of the bread on top and toast on a hot griddle for 5 minutes or until lightly brown. Turn bread over and toast another 5 minutes pressing gently with a spatula. Cut and serve warm.

WINE
RECOMMENDATION:

Chardonnay

Picnic Panini

This alternate panini uses the same ingredients as the panini
recipe on opposite page but a different method, making it
more appropriate for cooking a day in advance.

Serves 4

1 loaf ciabatta, foccacia, or
  baguette style bread, halved
  lengthwise
$^1/_2$ cup (118 ml) extra virgin
  olive oil
1 clove garlic, mashed
1 tablespoon chopped fresh
  Italian parsley
1 tablespoon chopped fresh basil

Pinch salt
$^1/_4$ pound (113 g) sliced prosciutto
$^1/_4$ pound (113 g) sliced fontina
  cheese
$^1/_4$ cup (60 g) sliced roasted red
  peppers
$^1/_2$ cup (113 g) fresh arugula
  (rocket) leaves or spinach

It is best to use large round foccacia bread, either 1 large or
2 small. Brush on olive oil mixture. Layer on meats and cheeses and
replace top half of bread. If using a smaller loaf, place it on a dinner
plate and invert another dinner plate over the top of the loaf. If using
a larger loaf, do the same with baking sheets. Place the covered panini in the refrigerator and put a heavy object, such as a brick or
canned goods, on the top of the plate or baking sheet to weigh the
loaf down for at least 2 hours, but best overnight.

Chef's Notes:

Eat the deliciously flattened panini for a picnic with a variety
of wines and cheeses. Remember to bring along an assortment
of fresh seasonal fruit, especially grapes, and a variety
of olives to round out your summer picnic.

WINE
RECOMMENDATION:

Sauvignon Blanc
or
Zinfandel

Mushroom and Herb-Stuffed Veal Chops

This can be served with Roasted Red Pepper Sauce on page 48.

Serves 4

4 (6 to 8 ounce/170 to 225 g) veal chops, each with pocket cut into chop (request butcher do this)
1 tablespoon butter
1 tablespoon olive oil
1 small yellow onion, chopped
2 cloves garlic, mashed
1 red bell pepper, diced
1 pound (450 g) mixed fresh mushrooms, finely chopped

1 tablespoon chopped fresh parsley
1 tablespoon chopped fresh thyme
$^1/_2$ teaspoon dry mustard
2 tablespoons Chardonnay
$^1/_4$ cup (28 g) fine bread crumbs
2 tablespoons grated Parmesan cheese
Salt and pepper to taste

Put veal chops in a shallow roasting pan. In a large skillet, add butter and olive oil. Cook onion, garlic, and bell pepper until soft. Add mushrooms and sauté 7 minutes. Add parsley, thyme, dry mustard, and Chardonnay. Simmer until moisture evaporates, about 5 minutes. Remove from heat and cool. Meanwhile, preheat broiler. Add bread crumbs and Parmesan cheese to cooled mushroom mixture. Add salt and pepper to taste. Stuff the mixture into pockets cut in each veal chop. Broil chops 5 to 7 minutes each side, until medium.

WINE RECOMMENDATION:

Chardonnay

Pounded Veal Chops

Serves 4

MARINADE:
2 tablespoons olive oil
Juice of $\frac{1}{2}$ lemon
2 tablespoons Chardonnay
1 tablespoon Worcestershire sauce
  (preferably white)
2 tablespoons chopped fresh
  Italian parsley
1 tablespoon chopped fresh thyme
1 teaspoon chopped capers

1 teaspoon dry mustard
2 cloves garlic, mashed
Salt to taste
White pepper to taste

VEAL:
4 veal chops, lightly pounded
$\frac{1}{2}$ cup (57 g) fine bread crumbs
2 tablespoons butter
2 tablespoons olive oil

For the marinade, in a shallow dish, mix together olive oil, lemon juice, Chardonnay, Worcestershire sauce, parsley, thyme, capers, dry mustard, garlic, salt, and white pepper.

For the veal, place chops into marinade and marinate chops for 1 hour.

Preheat oven to 300°F (150°C). Dredge the chops in the fine bread crumbs. In a skillet, heat butter and oil over medium-high to high heat. Brown chops on both sides until very golden brown, about 5 minutes each side. Remove to platter and place in oven for about 20 minutes. In the same pan, add remaining marinade and quickly reduce sauce. Spoon sauce over veal chops before serving.

WINE
RECOMMENDATION:

Chardonnay

Boneless Leg of Lamb

Serves 4 to 6

1 lamb leg, have butcher bone
  and fillet open
$^1/_4$ cup (60 ml) olive oil
$^3/_4$ cup (180 ml) Merlot
1 tablespoon Dijon mustard
2 tablespoons chopped fresh
  rosemary

2 tablespoons chopped Italian
  parsley
4 cloves garlic, chopped
Salt to taste
Generous amount coarse black
  pepper

Preheat grill, or oven to 375°F (190°C). Combine all ingredients except lamb. Rub completely over lamb leg. Let stand for 2 hours. This is best grilled over charcoal, but will do fine cooked in oven, until rare, or until meat thermometer registers 140°F (60°C). To serve, cut thinly across the grain and fan out on a plate.

Marinated Rack-of-Lamb

Serves 4

2 tablespoons olive oil
1 tablespoon balsamic vinegar
2 tablespoons red wine such
  as Zinfandel or Merlot
1 bay leaf, crushed
1 tablespoon each chopped fresh
  rosemary, thyme, Italian parsley

$^1/_4$ teaspoon freshly ground black
  pepper
$^1/_4$ teaspoon salt
$^1/_2$ teaspoon dry mustard
2 lamb racks, have the butcher
  "French" them (cut the excess
  fat off the ribs and back)

In a large zip-lock bag, mix all the ingredients together. Add lamb racks and rub marinade around the meat. Refrigerate overnight. Grill or oven roast to rare, until temperature on meat thermometer registers 140°F (60°).

WINE
RECOMMENDATION:

Merlot
or
Zinfandel

Marinated Rack-of-Lamb

Tuscan Steak

*Typically in Tuscany these steaks are simply prepared with garlic,
salt, and pepper, then a squeeze of lemon to finish. The meat
is always cooked rare and the steak is usually a T-bone cut.
Porterhouse, rib steak or even sirloin would do nicely.
If you like your steaks anything beyond medium rare use
the rib cut. It will stay tender even when well done.*

Serves 4

4 (6 to 8 ounce/170 to 225 g)
  T-bone or rib steaks
3 cloves garlic, chopped
Salt to taste
Generous amount freshly ground
  black pepper
2 tablespoons olive oil
1 tablespoon chopped fresh
  Italian parsley

1 teaspoon chopped fresh oregano,
  or $^1/_2$ teaspoon dried
$^1/_2$ teaspoon dry mustard
1 tablespoon balsamic vinegar
2 tablespoons Cabernet
  Sauvignon
1 lemon, cut in wedges

Place steaks into a shallow dish. Using a fork, mash garlic with
salt and pepper. Add oil, parsley, oregano, dry mustard, vinegar, and
wine. Mix well with fork to form a paste. Rub over steaks and let
marinate 30 minutes to 1 hour. Grill to desired doneness. Squeeze
lemon juice over steaks before serving.

WINE
RECOMMENDATION:

*Cabernet
Sauvignon*

Tuscan Steak

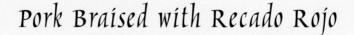

Pork Braised with Recado Rojo

*With thanks to Christine Keff of Fandango
for sharing her recipe and time.*

Serves 4 to 6

5 pounds (2.25 kg) pork butt,
  in one piece
1 large banana leaf
1 cup recado paste (opposite page)

¹/₂ cup (118 ml) lime juice
³/₄ cup (180 ml) orange juice,
  plus additional for deglazing

Mix the recado paste with fruit juices and set aside. Preheat oven to 200°F (95°C). Over an open flame, toast the banana leaf until it turns shiny, about 5 seconds. Line the bottom of a roasting pan with the banana leaf, draping the excess over the sides. Set the pork butt on the banana leaf and pour the recado mixture over it, rubbing it into the meat, (It's a good idea to wear rubber gloves while doing this as the paste stains skin.)

Fold the leaf over the meat and cover the roasting pan tightly with foil. Bake for six hours. Take the meat from the oven and let cool slightly, then shred the meat into bite-size pieces. The pan can be deglazed with orange juice to make a sauce for the pork.

WINE
RECOMMENDATION:

*Merlot
Syrah
or
Pinot Noir*

Recado Paste

Serves 4 to 6

2 cups (225 g) achiote seeds
  (annatto)
9 whole cloves
9 whole allspice berries
2 teaspoons whole cumin seed

5 bay leaves
4 teaspoons dried oregano
2 tablespoons salt
3 teaspoons chopped garlic

Put the achiote seeds in a small saucepan and cover with
1" (2.5 cm) water. Bring to a boil and simmer until the seeds are
very soft, about 20 minutes, strain and reserve the cooking liquid. Put
the softened seeds and the rest of the ingredients in a blender and add
just enough liquid to make a paste about the thickness of oatmeal.
Blend for 5 minutes or longer, until the paste is fairly smooth.

Chef's Notes:

*Achiote seeds come from the annato tree. They are
small and reddish in color. They are pronounced
"ah-chee-oh-tay" and you will find them where
you buy Latin American grocery items.*

WINE
RECOMMENDATION:

Merlot
Syrah
or
Pinot Noir

Potted Beef

*This is my sister's favorite that I had to have
and couldn't leave alone. Here's to M.J.*

Serves 4 to 6

3 pounds (1.35 kg) boneless beef
  chuck roast
Flour, for dredging
2 tablespoons olive oil
2 medium onions, chopped
2 cloves garlic, chopped
2 carrots, grated
1 or 2 Roma tomatoes, chopped
2 bay leaves
1 rosemary sprig
2 thyme sprigs
1 can (10$^{3}/_{4}$ ounce/300 g) golden
  cream of mushroom soup

$^{1}/_{2}$ cup (118 ml) Cabernet
  Sauvignon
$^{1}/_{2}$ cup (118 ml) water or stock
$^{1}/_{2}$ teaspoon dry mustard
1 teaspoon Dijon mustard
Salt and pepper to taste
1 pound (450 g) mushrooms, sliced
2 tablespoons butter
1 pound (450 g) cooked egg
  noodles or fettucine
Chopped fresh Italian parsley,
  for garnish

Preheat oven to 325°F (160°C). In a Dutch oven or ovenproof
pot with lid, dust beef roast with flour and brown in olive oil over
medium-high heat on all sides. Remove meat and sauté the onions,
garlic, and carrots until soft. Add tomatoes and simmer 2 more minutes. Add bay leaves, rosemary, thyme, soup, wine, water or stock,
dry mustard, and Dijon mustard. Add salt and pepper to taste.

Return meat to the pot, cover and cook in oven for 30 minutes.
In the meantime, sauté mushrooms with butter over medium-high
heat until brown. Turn the roast over and add mushrooms, cover
and cook another 45 minutes. Uncover the pot, stir and cook another
20 minutes or until roast is fork tender. Remove meat to a platter,
spoon some sauce over meat. Toss sauce with pasta-like wide egg
noodles, fettuccine, or pappardelle noodles. Garnish meat and pasta
with parsley.

W ine
Recommendation:

*Cabernet
Sauvignon
or
Meritage Red*

Side Dishes

Chardonnay and Mushrooms

Serves 4

2 pounds (900 g) whole button
  mushrooms, cleaned
$1/4$ cup (60 ml) olive oil
2 tablespoons Chardonnay
Juice of 1 lemon
4 cloves garlic, mashed
1 tablespoon chopped fresh basil
1 tablespoon chopped fresh
  Italian parsley

1 tablespoon chopped fresh
  oregano
$1/8$ teaspoon cumin
$1/8$ teaspoon paprika
$1/2$ teaspoon dry mustard
Salt to taste

Mix all ingredients together and marinate mushrooms at least 30 minutes. Sauté in hot skillet for 3 to 4 minutes until brown.

Fresh Grilled Asparagus

Serves 4

1 pound (450 g) fresh asparagus
2 tablespoons extra virgin
  olive oil

Salt to taste
Freshly ground black pepper
  to taste

Preheat barbecue. Clean and trim the asparagus. Place in a shallow dish and sprinkle with oil, salt, and black pepper. Lay asparagus directly on the barbecue crosswise. Grill over medium coals about 3 minutes each side. Serve with lemon wedges.

Eggplant and Mozzarella Casserole

This also makes an excellent vegetarian main dish.

Serves 4

2 medium eggplants (aubergines), cut into $1/2$" (1.25 cm) slices

2 tablespoons olive oil, for frying

3 large tomatoes, cut into $1/3$" (8 mm) round slices

1 large yellow onion, thinly sliced

3 cloves garlic, finely chopped

1 pound (450 g) fresh mozzarella, thinly sliced

2 tablespoons chopped fresh basil

2 tablespoons coarsely chopped fresh oregano

Salt and pepper to taste

2 tablespoons tomato paste

$1/3$ cup (80 ml) Sauvignon Blanc

$1/4$ cup (57 g) grated Parmesan cheese

2 tablespoons extra virgin olive oil, for garnish

Freshly grated black pepper

Preheat oven to 375°F (190°C). Lightly salt both sides of sliced eggplant and let stand about 20 minutes. This will draw out the bitter juices. Pat dry with paper towel. Brown very quickly in olive oil on both sides. You may have to add a bit more oil since the eggplant will absorb much of it. Remove eggplant and quickly sauté the garlic and onion until just wilted.

In an ovenproof baking pan, place one layer of eggplant, one layer of sliced tomato, a little sliced onion, some mozzarella, sprinkle on some of the basil and oregano. Lightly salt and pepper. Repeat this process until you have 3 layers. Mix tomato paste with Sauvignon Blanc and pour around the edges of the dish. Bake for approximately 20 minutes or until eggplant is very tender. Remove from oven and sprinkle on grated Parmesan cheese. Return to oven for another 5 minutes.

To serve, drizzle a little extra virgin olive oil over the top and grind a generous amount of black pepper.

WINE RECOMMENDATION:

Sauvignon Blanc

Gorgonzola Mashed Potatoes

Serves 4

2 pounds (900 g) new red
  potatoes, halved
4 large whole cloves garlic
¼ pound (113 g) Gorgonzola
  cheese

¼ cup (60 ml) half-and-half
2 tablespoons olive oil
Salt and pepper to taste

    Place potato and garlic cloves in a saucepan with enough water
to cover. Add salt and cook until tender. Drain and add the cheese,
half-and-half, and oil. Mash by hand; an electric mixer will make
the potatoes too gummy. Season with salt and pepper to taste.

Pistou

*This makes a different "pesto" and can be used in the same way.
It's great for topping fresh sliced tomatoes.*

Serves 4

1 cup (236 ml) fresh basil leaves
1 cup (236 ml) fresh Italian parsley
¼ cup (60 ml) fresh oregano leaves
3 cloves garlic
3 green onions

2 tablespoons extra virgin olive oil
Drop balsamic vinegar
Pinch salt
2 tablespoons grated Parmesan
  cheese

    Hand chop the basil, parsley, oregano, garlic, and green onions
together on a chopping board. Place in bowl and add olive oil,
balsamic vinegar, salt, and Parmesan cheese. Stir and let stand for
15 minutes before serving.

Pan-Roasted Peppers and Onions

This is a nice accompaniment to grilled meats.

Serves 4

1 large red bell pepper, julienned	2 cloves garlic, thinly sliced
1 large yellow bell pepper, julienned	2 tablespoons olive oil
	Salt to taste
1 large yellow onion, julienned	1 teaspoon balsamic vinegar

In a nonstick skillet, slowly sauté the peppers, onion, and garlic in olive oil over medium heat, stirring frequently. Cook for 20 minutes until vegetables are soft. Turn up the heat slightly and lightly brown, watching so they do not burn. Add salt and balsamic vinegar. Lower the heat and cook another 5 minutes.

WINE
RECOMMENDATION:

Sauvignon Blanc
or
Zinfandel

Potato, Spinach, and Salmon

*This is a dish I cooked with Michael Romano at the
Union Square Cafe. It's still one of my favorites!*

Serves 4

POTATOES:

4 purple potatoes, sliced ¹/₄"
(6 mm) thick rounds

4 yellow Finnish potatoes, sliced
¹/₄" (6 mm) thick rounds

4 red potatoes, sliced ¹/₄"
(6 mm) thick rounds

2 yellow onions, thinly sliced

1 fennel bulb, thinly sliced

2 cloves garlic, chopped

1 cup (225 g) chopped Roma
tomatoes

2 cups (475 ml) chicken stock

¹/₄ cup (60 ml) Chardonnay

2 tablespoons chopped fresh parsley

2 tablespoons chopped fresh
oregano

SALMON:

4 (4 to 5 ounce/113 to 140 g)
salmon fillets, cut on bias

Olive oil

Salt to taste

White pepper to taste

SPINACH:

2 tablespoons olive oil

1 clove garlic, mashed

2 bunches spinach, cleaned
and rinsed

1 lemon, cut into wedges,
for garnish

For the potatoes, in a skillet, sauté potatoes in batches
with onion, fennel, and garlic in olive oil until onions begin to wilt.
Add tomatoes and sauté another 5 minutes. Add chicken stock,
Chardonnay, parsley, and oregano. Cover and simmer 45 minutes
or until potatoes are tender.

For the salmon, rub fillets with olive oil, and salt and pepper.
In a separate pan, sauté fillets on a very hot heat for 3 minutes each
side. Remove and keep warm.

For the spinach, heat oil in sauté pan used for salmon and lightly
brown garlic. Add spinach and sauté for about 3 to 4 minutes, until
spinach wilts.

On a warm dinner plate, spread out the sautéed
potatoes and onions. Top with spinach. Place salmon
on spinach and garnish with lemon.

WINE
RECOMMENDATION:

Chardonnay

Ratatouille

Serves 4

2 tablespoons olive oil
1 eggplant (aubergine), cut into
  1" (2.5 cm) squares
1 large yellow onion, chopped
1 red bell pepper, chopped
1 yellow bell pepper, chopped
4 cloves garlic, mashed
2 tablespoons chopped fresh
  Italian parsley

2 tablespoons chopped fresh
  oregano
1 teaspoon cumin
Salt and pepper to taste
1/4 cup (60 ml) Merlot
2 tablespoons tomato paste

In a skillet with olive oil, sauté the eggplant, onion, and red and yellow peppers until wilted. Add garlic and continue to sauté another 5 minutes. Add parsley, oregano, cumin, and salt and pepper and mix thoroughly. Mix Merlot with tomato paste and stir into the ratatouille. Cover and cook over low heat until very soft.

Sautéed Greens

Serves 4

2 tablespoons olive oil
1 clove garlic, mashed
1 large head escarole (curly leaf
  endive)

Black pepper to taste
2 tablespoons grated Parmesan
  cheese, for garnish

In a large skillet, heat olive oil and lightly brown garlic. Add escarole and sauté quickly for 3 minutes or until wilted. Cover and simmer over low heat, about 12 minutes. Place on serving dish and sprinkle with ground black pepper and grated Parmesan cheese.

Sautéed Snow Peas

*This is a very simple, but delicious dish to serve
using the delicate peas that are in abundance in the spring.*

Serves 4

¹/₄ pound (113 g) snow peas
1 tablespoon peanut oil

1 teaspoon soy sauce

Sauté snow peas very quickly in peanut oil and soy sauce, until just heated through.

Sautéed Rapini

Serves 4

1 bunch (1.5 pounds/675 g) rapini
  (Chinese broccoli)
3 ounces (85 g) coarsely chopped
  pancetta (Italian bacon) or
  3 slices bacon

2 tablespoons olive oil
2 cloves garlic, thinly sliced
1 teaspoon balsamic vinegar
Salt to taste
Coarsely ground pepper to taste

In a 3 quart (3 l) pot, bring lightly salted water to a boil. Trim thick stalks from rapini. Blanch in boiling salted water for 2 minutes. Remove and cool in an ice bath. Chill. In a large skillet, sauté the pancetta in olive oil till crisp. If using bacon slices do not add olive oil. Add garlic and sauté until soft, not brown. Add vinegar to saucepan, place rapini in saucepan, and toss until warmed. Finish with salt and ground pepper.

WINE
RECOMMENDATION:

Sauvignon Blanc

Potato Lasagna

This style of casserole is found in the Alps—
whether it be Italian, French or Swiss Alps.
Full flavored wine complements this rich, warming dish.

Serves 4

2 yellow onions, thinly sliced

1 tablespoon olive oil

Butter, for greasing baking dish

2 pounds (900 g) russet potatoes,
  peeled, thinly sliced

1 pound (450 g) thinly sliced ham,
  such as Black Forest or
  French Jambon

1 pound (450 g) shredded fontina
  cheese or Gruyère cheese

3 tomatoes, thinly sliced
  (preferably oven-roasted)

$^1/_2$ cup (118 ml) chopped
  fresh basil

Salt to taste

White pepper to taste

2 cups (475 ml) milk, scalded

$^1/_4$ cup (60 ml) chicken stock,
  if necessary

Preheat oven to 350°F (180°C). In sauté pan, gently cook onions in olive oil until soft. Grease baking dish with butter. Place a layer of potato in the baking dish. Top potato layer with individual layers of onion, ham, cheese, and tomato. Sprinkle tomato layer with fresh basil, salt, and pepper. Repeat layering until dish is full, which should be approximately three layers of each filling. Finish construction with a layer of cheese. Pour in scalded milk and cover the dish with foil. Bake in oven for 20 minutes. Remove foil. Check liquid; if dish seems too dry, add chicken stock. Continue to bake another 20 minutes or until top layer of cheese is brown and potatoes are tender.

WINE
RECOMMENDATION:

Chardonnay
Pinot Noir
or
Meritage

Stuffed Potatoes

This can also be served as a main dinner dish or as a cold day lunch.

Serves 4

POTATOES:
2 large whole baking potatoes
2 slices bacon (optional)

STUFFING:
1 cup (225 g) ricotta
$^1/_2$ cup green onions, chopped
4 tablespoons basil pesto
Salt and pepper to taste

Preheat oven to 350°F (180°C). Pierce potatoes with a fork. Wrap 1 piece bacon around potato and wrap in foil. Bake for 1 hour.

When potatoes are cooked, cut in half lengthwise. Remove potato from skins and place in a bowl. Add ricotta cheese, onions, and pesto and mix well. Restuff the potato skins and return to oven for 10 minutes.

Sweet Red Pepper Purée

Serves 4

2 tablespoons olive oil
2 red bell peppers, thinly sliced
2 large yellow onions, thinly sliced

3 cloves garlic, mashed
$^1/_2$ teaspoon red pepper flakes
Salt to taste

In a skillet, heat olive oil over medium heat. Sauté peppers, onion and garlic, and then season with pepper flakes and salt. Reduce heat to low and cook, stirring occasionally, until very soft, about 30 minutes. Purée in blender until smooth.

Thai-Style Asparagus
Serves 4

$^1/_2$ pound (225 g) asparagus, trimmed
$^1/_4$ pound (113 g) shiitake mushrooms, sliced
1 yellow onion, sliced
1 tablespoon peanut oil
$^1/_2$ teaspoon sesame oil

3 cloves garlic, thinly sliced
1 tablespoon grated fresh ginger
$^1/_4$ cup (60 ml) chicken stock
1 teaspoon Thai chili sauce
1 teaspoon soy sauce
1 teaspoon chopped fresh cilantro

In a wok or skillet, sauté asparagus, shiitake mushrooms, and onion in peanut and sesame oils until just tender. Add garlic and ginger and sauté 3 more minutes. Add chicken stock, chili sauce, soy sauce, and cilantro. Stir well. Serve over rice.

Merlot-Plum Chutney

Use this versatile sauce to accompany all types of meat,
whether grilled, roasted, or smoked.

1 teaspoon peanut oil
1 red onion, julienned
1 tablespoon grated fresh ginger

$^1/_4$ cup (60 ml) Merlot
2 cups (475 ml) sliced fresh plums
Pinch orange zest

In a skillet, over medium heat, add peanut oil and sauté onion and ginger for 2 to 3 minutes. Add Merlot, plums, and orange zest. Cover, reduce heat, and simmer until plums are quite mushy and sauce has thickened.

Stone Fruit Relish

Serve this relish with fish, particularly grilled salmon or grilled ahi.

2 peaches, peeled and diced
2 plums, peeled and diced
2 nectarines, peeled and diced

Juice of 1 lime
1 tablespoon chopped fresh
  cilantro

Mix all relish ingredients together and blend well. Let stand for 30 minutes.

Braised Slaw

Serves 4 to 6

1 small head red cabbage, shredded	1 sprig thyme
1 tablespoon olive oil	1 tablespoon apple cider vinegar
4 juniper berries	1 tablespoon red wine vinegar
4 whole peppercorns	1 heaping tablespoon brown sugar
3 bay leaves	1 cup (236 ml) chicken stock
	Pinch salt

In a large 6 quart (3 l) pot, heat oil over medium heat. Add juniper berries, peppercorns, bay leaves, and thyme. Stir briefly to release the fragrances of the spices. Add apple cider vinegar, red wine vinegar, chicken stock, and brown sugar. Bring to a boil and stir until sugar dissolves. Add cabbage, and turn heat down to a simmer. Cover and cook 10 to 12 minutes, stirring occasionally until cabbage is cooked but still slightly crisp.

Veggie Kabobs
Serves 4

BASTE:
¼ cup (60 ml) extra virgin olive oil
Juice of 1 lemon
2 tablespoons Sauvignon Blanc
⅛ cup chopped fresh Italian
  parsley
2 tablespoons chopped fresh
  oregano
3 cloves garlic, chopped
½ teaspoon cumin
½ teaspoon dry mustard
Salt and pepper to taste

VEGETABLES:
1 eggplant (aubergine), cut into
  1½" (3.75 cm) cubes
2 yellow crookneck squash, cut
  into 1" (2.5 cm) cubes
2 yellow onions, cut into
  1" (2.5 cm) cubes
8 whole large button mushrooms
2 sweet red bell peppers, cut into
  1" (2.5 cm) cubes

Mix all baste ingredients together and set aside. Skewer all vegetables and baste kabobs. Grill, barbecue, or broil the kabobs until vegetables are tender, turning frequently.

Desserts

Raspberry Mousse
Serves 4

RASPBERRY MOUSSE:
$^1/_2$ cup (118 ml) whipping cream,
   whipped until stiff peaks form
$^1/_2$ cup (113 g) sour cream
1 cup (236 ml) fresh or frozen
   raspberries (reserve some whole
   berries as garnish)
Squeeze of lemon juice
2 tablespoons sugar
Mint leaves, for garnish

COOKIE CRUST:
2 cups (60 cookies) vanilla wafers
   (1 package wine biscuits)
3 to 4 tablespoons butter, melted

For the mousse, fold whipped cream into sour cream, add
berries, lemon juice, and sugar.

For the crust, in a blender or food processor, chop cookies until
fine. Add butter and mix until cookie crumbs absorb butter. Press the
cookie "dough" into small sorbet cups much like a pie shell.

Pour raspberry mousse mixture into crust and refrigerate for
1 hour. Garnish each with raspberries and mint leaves.

**WINE
RECOMMENDATION:**

*Late Harvest
Riesling*

Raspberry Mousse

Fresh Strawberry Torte

Serves 4

4 puff pastry shells
2 cups (450 g) strawberries
¼ cup (60 ml) berry liqueur
1 teaspoon sugar
1 teaspoon lemon zest

2 cups (475 ml) crème anglaise
   or custard sauce (p. 124)
½ cup (118 ml) apricot preserves,
   melted

Preheat oven to 350°F (180°C). Bake pastry shells 7 minutes, until brown. Marinate strawberries in berry liqueur, sugar, and lemon zest, for at least 20 minutes. Fill pastry shells with crème anglaise and cover with marinated berries. Glaze with melted apricot preserves.

Strawberries Fragole All'Aceto Balsamico

I first had this dish in Verona in 1977, but could not figure out what they had done to make the berries taste so incredible. After some research, I found that it was the balsamic vinegar that really awakened the berries. Grinding the bit of fresh ground pepper over each serving may seem startling, but just try it. This recipe also works well if the berries are not as ripe as you would like.

Serves 4

1 pound (450 g) strawberries,
   halved (avoid washing if possible)
1 tablespoon granulated sugar

1 to 1½ tablespoons balsamic
   vinegar
Small grinding of black pepper

Sprinkle the berries with sugar and let stand about 1 hour. Add balsamic vinegar and toss gently. Let stand another 15 minutes. Finish by grinding black pepper over the top.

WINE
RECOMMENDATION:

*Late Harvest
Riesling*

Fresh Strawberry Torte

Cherry Strudel

*This dish is something I can remember eating as a child,
especially during fresh cherry season. Try to find the slightly
tart pitted pie cherries, although any variety will do.*

Serves 4

4 cups (900 kg) cherries,
  pitted
¹/₃ cup (75 g) sugar
¹/₂ cup (57 g) flour
¹/₂ cup (113 g) chopped hazelnuts

Pinch cinnamon
¹/₈ teaspoon orange zest
¹/₂ cup (113 g) butter, melted
5 sheets phyllo dough
Powdered sugar, for garnish

Preheat oven to 350°F (180°C). Mix together cherries, sugar,
flour, hazelnuts, cinnamon, and orange zest.

Brush butter on phyllo sheet. Top with another phyllo sheet
and butter again. Do this for 5 layers. Place cherry mixture on
phyllo dough and turn over edges. Roll up and butter top of phyllo
"log." Bake in oven until brown, 15 to 20 minutes. Cool. Dust with
powdered sugar before serving.

WINE
RECOMMENDATION:

*Late Harvest
Riesling*

Pear and Lychee Nut Sorbet

*Lychee nuts and pears are a natural complement
to the honey sweetness of the Late Harvest Riesling
and it makes a great dessert combination.*

Serves 4

1 can (11 ounces/329 g) drained
  lychee nuts
3 pears, peeled, cored, and sliced

1 tablespoon lemon juice
$^{1}/_{4}$ cup (57 g) sugar
2 tablespoons Late Harvest Riesling

Place all ingredients in a blender and blend well. Use gelato machine according to manufacturer's instructions and keep frozen.

Raspberry-Lemon Sorbet

Try a sparkling white wine like Blanc de Blanc with this sorbet.

Serves 4

3 cups (700 g) fresh raspberries
2 tablespoons lemon juice
1 cup (236 ml) water
$^{1}/_{2}$ cup (113 g) sugar

$^{1}/_{4}$ teaspoon lemon zest
2 tablespoons Late Harvest
  Riesling
2 large egg whites

In food processor or blender, purée berries and lemon juice. In saucepan, add water and sugar, dissolve sugar over low heat; let cool. Mix in berry purée, lemon zest, and Riesling. Whip egg whites to firm and fold in. Use ice cream maker and freeze until firm.

Chef's Notes:

*To make ice cream without an ice-cream maker, pour the
mixture into a shallow plastic container and freeze 3 to 4
hours. Beat the mixture and return to freezer for another
3 hours. Beat again and store in the freezer.*

Espresso Tíramísù

This is a slightly different take on classic tiramisù.
There are always a variety of ways to make a recipe,
and this one uses espresso, a Pacific Northwest favorite.
The custard is best made one day ahead.

Serves 6 to 8

CUSTARD:

6 egg yolks, slightly beaten
6 tablespoons sugar
Pinch salt
2 cups (475 ml) milk or
  half-and-half, scalded
¼ cup (60 ml) of Marsala wine
8 ounces (225 g) fresh mascarpone
  cheese

BASE:

24 ladyfingers
1 cup (236 ml) strongly brewed
  espresso
1 cup (236 ml) heavy cream,
  whipped firm
Solid bittersweet chocolate,
  for garnish
Frozen raspberries, for garnish
Fresh small mint leaves
½ cup crumbled amaretto cookies

For the custard, use a double boiler, or saucepan with a stainless
steel bowl set on top, half full with water, and bring water to barely
boiling. Put eggs, sugar and salt into bowl, and whisk until blended.
Stir until eggs begin to thicken and are well blended. Slowly pour in
scalded milk, small amounts at a time, until blended and continue to
whisk until thick, about 7 to 8 minutes. Once thickened, add Marsala
wine and mascarpone cheese and whisk until smooth. Place bowl in
refrigerator until firm, preferably overnight.

For the base, quickly dip ladyfingers in espresso. Turn each face
down and line bottom and sides of a glass serving bowl or decorative
bowl. Spread ⅓ cup whipped cream on top of ladyfingers. Pour
firmed, chilled custard on top; bowl will be almost full. Top with
remaining whipped cream, and spread evenly. Use a potato peeler
to shave delicate twirls of the solid bittersweet chocolate, and sprinkle
on top. Dot with berries, and place 2 small mint
leaves next to each berry. Sprinkle with amaretto
cookie crumbs to finish.

WINE
RECOMMENDATION:

Riesling
or
Tawny Port

Tarte Tatin

Serves 6 to 8

CRUST:
1³/₄ cups (200 g) flour
¹/₂ cup (113 g) butter
6 tablespoons sugar
Lemon zest from ¹/₂ lemon
3 egg yolks
1 tablespoon brandy

FILLING:
10 to 12 apples, Granny Smith
  and Golden Delicious, mixed
2 cups (450 g) powdered sugar
4 tablespoons (57 g) butter, melted
Juice of 2 lemons
1 tablespoon vanilla

For the crust, place flour, butter, sugar, and lemon zest in a food processor, and process until blended. Add the egg yolks and brandy and process until the dough forms a ball. Remove from food processor and shape dough into a disc. Wrap in plastic and refrigerate until chilled, about 1 hour.

For the filling, preheat oven to 375°F (180°C). Peel, core and slice each apple into 8 even slices. Sprinkle the bottom of a 12" (30 cm) ovenproof, nonstick skillet with some of the powdered sugar. Place some of the apples in a decorative pattern on the powdered sugar. Repeat with additional layers of powdered sugar and apples until apples are all layered. Drizzle the lemon juice, butter, and vanilla over the apples.

Cover the pan and place it on the stove over low heat. Allow the apples to cook gently until the sugar in the bottom has started to caramelize. (This may take longer if the apples are watery.)

Meanwhile, roll out the pastry dough into a round, slightly larger than the apple pan, about ¹/₈" (3 mm) thick. Refrigerate until apples are chilled. Cover the apple mixture with the pastry dough and bake 15 to 20 minutes. Remove tarte from the oven and invert onto a plate. Serve warm.

WINE
RECOMMENDATION:

*Late Harvest
Riesling*

Stuffed Apple Bowls
Serves 4

4 tart apples, such as pippin or
  Granny Smith
¹/₂ lemon
¹/₂ cup (113 g) butter
¹/₂ cup (113 g) packed brown sugar
¹/₃ cup (80 ml) orange concentrate
¹/₂ cup (118 ml) Johannisberg
  Riesling, divided

1 cup (225 g) chopped mixed
  dried fruits, such as apricots,
  dates, and figs
¹/₂ cup (113 g) chopped hazelnuts
  (filberts) or walnuts
Scant ¹/₈ teaspoon each of
  cinnamon, nutmeg, and clove

Scoop out core of apples to make a small bowl suitable for
stuffing. Rub apples with lemon to prevent browning while preparing
stuffing. Preheat oven to 350°F (180°C). In a saucepan, melt butter.
Add brown sugar, orange juice, and ¹/₄ cup wine, and stir until brown
sugar is melted. Add chopped fruits and spices. Simmer until blended.
Stir in chopped nuts. With slotted spoon, remove nuts and dried
fruit. Reserve remaining liquid for basting. Stuff apple bowls with
simmered nut and fruit mixture. Place stuffed apples in buttered
baking dish. Pour the remaining ¹/₄ cup of wine around apples, and
bake in oven for 25 minutes, or until apples are tender to touch.
Baste frequently with reserved liquid.

WINE
RECOMMENDATION:

*Late Harvest
Riesling*

Zuccotto

*This is a great, mousse-like Italian chilled cake that I like
to serve around Easter when the first strawberries are out
to garnish the cake. In Italy, it's called a "beach ball cake."
This is a dessert that my two boys, Biagio and Dominic,
can eat all by themselves but normally it will serve six.*

Serves 6

2 rectangular or round sponge
  cakes (angel food cake)
3 tablespoons Frangelica Liqueur
  or brandy
3 cups (709 ml) whipping cream
$^1/_2$ cup finely chopped roasted
  hazelnuts, divided

$^1/_2$ tablespoon powdered sugar,
  divided
$^1/_2$ cup grated chocolate
2 tablespoons cocoa
Fresh strawberries, if available

Line a 10 to 12" round, stainless steel bowl with plastic wrap.
Cut sponge cake into $^1/_2$" layers and line the bowl with the cake.
Whip cream until very stiff. Divide cream in half. To one half of the
whipped cream, add half of the hazelnuts, half of the powdered
sugar and all of the grated chocolate; fold in completely. Sprinkle the
sponge cake in the bowl with the liqueur or brandy. Fill the cake-
lined bowl half full with the whipped cream mixture. If you have
fresh strawberries available, you can put a layer of sliced, fresh strawberries on top of the whipped cream mixture. To the remaining plain
whipped cream, add the remaining hazelnuts, powdered sugar, and
cocoa; fold in completely. Pour on top of the whipped cream mixture
and strawberries already in the bowl and smooth out. This should use
up all your cream mixture. Top with remaining sponge cake; cover
and refrigerate at least 2 hours or overnight.

When ready to serve, remove plastic wrap, invert bowl onto
serving plate and sprinkle top with powdered sugar and cocoa.

WINE
RECOMMENDATION:

*Late Harvest
Riesling*

Marinated Plums and Chilled Lychee Nuts

Serves 4

1 cup (236 ml) White Riesling
1 tablespoon sugar
¹/₄ teaspoon lemon zest
1 small stick cinnamon

1 pound (450 g) plums or prunes,
   pitted and quartered
2 cans (11 ounces/329 g) lychee
   nuts

Bring to a boil, White Riesling, sugar, lemon zest, and cinnamon stick. Add plums and simmer 5 minutes. Remove from heat and chill. Add lychee nuts and serve.

Stone Fruit Dessert

Serves 4

1 cup (225 g) sliced peaches
1 cup (225 g) sliced nectarines
1 cup (225 g) sliced plums or
   prunes
1 cup (225 g) pitted cherries

3 or 4 slices fresh ginger
2 tablespoons lemon juice
1 cup (225 g) Late Harvest
   Riesling
Sprigs of fresh mint (optional)

Toss together peaches, nectarines, plums, cherries, ginger, and lemon juice. Spoon into individual serving cups and pour Late Harvest Riesling over fruit. Refrigerate. Serve garnished with mint.

WINE
RECOMMENDATION:

Late Harvest
Riesling

The Perfect Finish
to the Perfect Pairing

Matching coffee to the end of a meal is very much
like pairing wine with food. It is, as with wine,
important to think of balancing the flavor of the
coffee with the overall flavor of the meal.

If you've just eaten a very rich meal, often a light
and refreshing high-acid coffee works wonders to
refresh the palate. Or, if you've just polished off
a rich and full dessert, you'd want to drink a dark
roast coffee. The strength, flavor, and bouquet of
coffee are determined not only by the bean variety
but also by the technique used to roast it, much
like with wine grapes. So, to make the perfect
ending to the perfect pairing of wine and food,
be adventurous and try your hand at matching
all varieties of coffee with your meal's end.

Index

Numbers in boldface indicate photos.

Index

Index